LET IT GO!

Virginia Harrison, Ph.D.

Let it Go!
by Virginia Harrison, Ph.D.

Printed in the United States of America

ISBN 9781615795468

www.xulonpress.com

~ Table of Contents ~

~ *Dedicated To* ~

This book is dedicated to my mother, Josephine Harrison, who always told me that I could do anything that I put my mind to. Mom, I love and thank you.

In Memory of

John Emory Harrison (father) who spoke negative words into my life and gave a hard discipline in my mouth yet told me in my late thirties, when I asked about his behavior toward me, that he saw something in me. Thanks, Daddy, for your insight into my life.

Shirley Harrison, my sister, best friend, and counselor (with spiritual wisdom). She was the wind beneath my wings. Thanks, Shirley, for being what I needed in my life.

Presiding Elder Doreatha Hawkins (West Virginia) and evangelist Ruby Crawford (Michigan), both spiritual mothers, who accepted me as part of their families. Thanks for allowing me to sit at your feet, to hear your wonderful experiences as my spiritual giants used by God to bless so many people. As I listened to you both sharing, I did not realize that one day I would be a preacher also. Thanks, Mother Hawkins and Mother Crawford, for making a tremendous impact in my life and making me proud to be one of your children.

~ Acknowledgement ~

I praise the Lord for blessing me with the talent, gift, vision and ability to write this book. It has been a long time in the developmental stage. However, to God be the glory for the great things that He has done, and is doing, in my life. The writing of this book has been therapeutic for me. As I wrote, I realized that I have let many things go—those things that used to truly bother me do not faze me now. But, as Jesus is still working on me, I will always hear these words in my ears—Let it go!

I thank my mother, Josephine Harrison, for her prayers, confidence in me, and for encouraging me about how greatly God is using me.

I thank my spiritual mothers who always shared their wisdom with me: Ms. Lillie Askew (Washington, DC), Ms. Jean Jackson (Maryland), and Ms. Harlie Wilmore (Maryland).

My heartfelt thanks goes out to my friends, without whose encouragement, loyalty, wisdom, and valuable insight, this book would have never become a reality. They have been a source of tremendous strength and encouragement to me personally throughout the years this book has been in the making and to them goes my deepest thanks and appreciation. When you try to thank everyone, the absence of some names is painfully obvious to whomever is omitted.

I praise the Lord for the people in this book. They came into my life for a reason, a specific season, or for a lifetime. Without you, I would not have the testimony that He is Jehovah-Jireh— my provider.

Disclaimer: The events in this book are true. However, some of the names have been changed to protect the identities of the individuals, colleges, and churches.

~ *Introduction* ~

Many times, we encounter trials in life that we believe will take us out of this world through a stress attack, heart attack, or some other ailment. Even though we say that we trust in the Lord, it does not necessarily mean that the anxiety or stress associated with the trial goes away. But, believing and trusting in the Lord in our spirit and heart, enables us to know that God will somehow work the situation out for our good.

"Trust in the Lord with all thine heart; and lean not unto thine own understanding. In all thy ways acknowledge him, and he shall direct thy paths." (Proverbs 3:5, 6, KJV)

Trusting God does not mean that we will not get any bruises and experience pain during the trial. What it means is that, the great and mighty God we serve will take the problem, when we cast the care upon Him, let it go, and allow Him to handle it.

I felt that God wanted me to write this book. I procrastinated and rationalized for years because I neither felt equipped to write a book, nor could I imagine that I had anything to add to a subject as familiar as that of "let it go". But the longer I put it off, the more convicted in my spirit I became. It really wasn't a question of whether I had anything to add or whether anyone would learn from what I had to say, the question was: "Is God telling me to write this book?" If He was, then I had to get on with the job of writing, or else be willing to suffer the consequences. I can tell you without fear of any skeptical response, that God told me to write this book. It was, and is an exercise in obedience. And when all else is said and done, that is exactly what this book if all about: obedience, the struggles I encountered in my life, and the difficulties I had in letting those struggles go.

The things you will read and the examples I will share with you are all real, either from my own life, or from the lives of others. Many of the things I have learned have come as a result of great pain. My life has not been easy, but it certainly has been blessed.

My life was stuck like glue to the pain associated with my trials, until I decided it profited me nothing to keep holding on. So eventually with the help of Jesus and a determination to move on, I let it (my past) go. I had difficulties releasing and walking away from my past because I did not want to repeat my mistakes. Sometimes it was comfortable to stay where I was because I did not know what would happen, if, I let it go. Would it get better or worse? I was afraid to take that chance. As a person who always wants to do my best at everything that I do, I tried to operate in a spirit of excellence. Maybe, in essence, I tried to be an overachiever, who was perfect. Failure at anything hurt, and caused me a lingering pain that took a long time to let go. Over time, I had to learn that one of the best things to do in life is to let some things go.

"Brethren, I count not myself to have apprehended: but this one thing I do, forgetting those things which are behind, and reaching forth unto those things which are before. I press toward the mark for the prize of the high calling of God in Christ Jesus." (Philippians 3:13, 14, KJV)

Everything (people and tangible/intangible things) that we encounter in life is not always meant to stay. I learned through many trials that some things were placed in my life only for a reason or a season. And, occasionally, something came into my life to stay. I finally realized the importance of putting things into the appropriate categories in my life so that I could let them run their assigned course in my life's journey.

After facing the difficulty of a failed marriage, and encountering confrontations with some family members and other relationships, I took a good long look at myself. Fueled probably by depression, I blamed myself for practically everything that happened in my life. I felt that if I blamed me, accepting the responsibility for failures in my life, it would make the pain go away and my life would flow in victory and peace again.

My hope is that my story will help to encourage you who are encountering pain as you go through trials and tribulations that it does not mean that you are not walking in victory and peace. Some of the worst trials I encountered, I walked through in peace because as the poem "Footprints in the Sand" communicates: God was carrying me.

"There hath no temptation taken you but such as is common to man: but God is faithful, who will not suffer you to be tempted above that ye are able; but will with the temptation also make a way to escape, that ye may be able to bear it." (I Corinthians 10:13, KJV)

God will not put any more on us than we can bear. When we think we are at the point of breaking, it is at that point that God carries us the rest of the way through the trial. Before God sees us giving up, throwing in the towel, allowing sickness or death to overcome us; He will turn down the heat in the fiery furnace. Ultimately, He doesn't want to destroy us, He wants the glory out of our lives:

"But we all, with open face beholding as in a glass the glory of the Lord, are changed into the same image from glory to glory, even as by the Spirit of the Lord."
(II Corinthians 3:18, KJV)

Warfare Within

At times in my life, I have felt like walking into a bar or liquor store to purchase liquor to deaden the pain and to forget the memory of the ordeal. I praise God that the following three scriptures help bring me through the trials. I kept quoting them, holding onto hope by the thread of these scriptures in my heart, and out of my mouth: Hebrews 13:5: "I will never leave thee, nor forsake thee" Psalm 37:25: "I have been young, and now am old; yet have I not seen the righteous forsaken, nor his seed begging bread."; and Psalms 37:23: "The steps of a good man are ordered by the LORD: and he delighted in his way."

Those scriptures were constantly spoken out of my mouth because the spiritual warfare within kept weakening me. Fighting for me was difficult. I felt like a boxer in a ring too weak to fight, but I did not throw in the towel, even though many times I felt like doing so. I finally let go of thinking "why were these things happening to me when I did not seek to hurt anyone but to help?"

I learned that being a peaceful person does not always mean that trouble and turbulence will not find me. Eventually, I put people and things into the appropriate category of life's encounters and moved on. I learned there are times I may not know or understand why the trial or tribulation happened, but I can always know that Jesus, God and the Holy Spirit were in the midst of the fire with me.

The Holy Spirit encouraged me many times to let go of my past, but I still had a problem releasing it. I needed to understand "why?" Sometimes, I got my answer and other times, I did not. I was being stretched in the area of trust, and learning to believe that God wanted me to depend upon Him. I had a stronghold in my life that seemed to be rooted in my past and I needed to know what to do to get my deliverance.

In the ministry, the Holy Spirit used me tremendously, under the anointing to assist people to receive their deliverance by revealing their past to them, helping them to forgive self and others, and other issues that only the Holy Spirit could reveal to me about them. Now, it was my turn. So, where was the person to help me to get a breakthrough? I cited some of the same deliverance words that the Holy Spirit gave me to give to others, but I could not get free from the stronghold of fear and insecurity. I prayed, fasted, cried and grieved a lot. One of my personality traits is to analyze and/or reason things out. I did a historical mapping of my life to see where the root of my problem started. I could not "let go."

I have learned the hard way that God has a plan for my life, and when I act in a fashion that is inconsistent with that plan, it can become very painful. The bottom line is obedience. God's plan for my life is too big for me to comprehend. I believe my life story and testimony will encourage you to let go of those things that hinders your spiritual growth and negatively affect your well-being so that you can move ahead until your breakthrough is manifested.

CHAPTER 1

MY CHILDHOOD

"Then the word of the LORD came unto me, saying,
Before I formed thee in the belly I knew thee; and before
thou camest forth out of the womb I sanctified thee, and
I ordained thee a prophet unto the nations."
(Jeremiah 1:4, 5, KJV)

I was reared on a farm in Prince George's County, Upper Marlboro, Maryland by my parents. From their union came seven children, only four of whom lived in the family home at one time because of the extreme differences in our age groupings. My three oldest siblings—Rachel, Melissa, and Joseph— are old enough to be my parents. My parents waited ten years before having their next child, Gregory. Three years later, they had my sister Sherita and then three years following that - me. My sister Jacquelyn came five years after me. I thought I was the baby of the family, until my brother Joseph brought my mother home from the hospital with my baby sister, Jacquelyn. I did not know that my mother was pregnant nor where she had been. Unlike children today with such knowledge of life, at the age of five I did not know anything about a woman having a baby. In fact, we did not discuss sex in our home—I learned about sex from friends at school, especially listening to the boys.

My parents worked hard to provide for our family. My father was a sharecropper farmer and my mother a domestic worker, cleaning the homes of several Caucasian families for many years. We lived in a three-bedroom rambler farmhouse. We had two wood burning stoves, one used for cooking and the other for heating the house. We also had an electric stove. We did not have indoor plumbing until I was about age nine. We got our water from a well and used it for washing clothes (with a scrub board or a wringer washing machine), bathing and cooking. Since we did not have indoor bathroom plumbing for many years, we used a portable receptacle for inside use and dumped it daily, and an outhouse for additional bathroom needs. But this was our home. This was my humble beginning.

Early every morning before I could go to school, I sat at the window watching Gregory and Sherita leaving home, walking to the bus stop. Our mailbox was located on Ritchie Marlboro Road, but we actually lived about one-and-a-half miles from the main road. Our nearest neighbor was an elderly couple: Mr. Oliver Robinson, whom we called Mr. Ollie and his companion, Ms. Isabel Belton. Mr. Ollie helped my father on the farm with the tobacco crop, and Ms. Isabel did domestic work for the Caucasian family that my father worked for as a sharecropper. Mr. Ollie and Ms. Isabel were a part of our family. Every Thursday night they came to our house to watch wrestling on television with my father, since they did not own a television.

We did not have some of the things that other families had such as fine modern cars, a modern home, or stylish clothes. But we never lacked for the things we needed. Most of the clothes we wore were second-hand, given to us by my mother's employers or an aunt, who lived in Washington, D.C., and who we considered to be financially comfortable.

My parents bought us clothes for Easter, back-to-school, and Christmas and seldom any other times. My mother usually bought Sherita and I the same outfits in different colors. I do not know why my mother dressed us alike; maybe, it was easier after she found something that she liked. She never dressed Jacquelyn like us because Jacqueline was in elementary school, it would have been odd to dress two teenagers like an elementary school age child.

Sherita and I slept in the same room alone for years, while Jacquelyn slept in a separate bed in our parent's room. When Jacquelyn was around age seven, our parents moved her into the bedroom with Sherita and me.

Life on the Farm

My father rose before the break of dawn to start his day on the farm growing tobacco for marketing and farming livestock. We never knew what it felt like to be hungry or without food because we grew our own vegetables, raised livestock (hogs and chickens) to slaughter for food, cows for milk, and horses to pull the farm plow for gardening and growing tobacco. My mother rose early each day to prepare breakfast for my father and his brother, Roscoe, who lived with our family for over 50 years until his death. Uncle Roscoe came to live with us after he got sick and needed constant care. She would have the food ready when they took their first break from the farm chores for breakfast. My mother prepared each meal for my father and uncle and set it before them on the table. Afterwards, she would prepare herself for work. She never learned to drive, so her employer had to pick her up for work. She always left us instructions to have the house cleaned before she returned home from work. She always prepared a full-course lunch for my father and the people who worked for him on the farm. Sherita or I just had to reheat and serve it.

The days that my mother worked, she left home after we left for school and returned before we came home. In the summer while we were out of school, we had to help our father in the tobacco field, in addition to our house chores. In my teenage years, I would write down everything that I had to do, and scratch it off my list upon completion so I could finish before the soap operas came on television at noon each day.

As I stated earlier, we lived about one and a half miles off the nearest road in a rural area. Our house was positioned between two roads, Ritchie Marlboro Road and Brown Station Road. We could see Brown Station Road from our back porch. There was no road or makeshift road leading to Brown Station Road from our house for several years. Therefore, we would only walk to Brown Station Road from our house if it was necessary. Later, Gregory talked with the bus driver and changed our bus stop from Ritchie Marlboro Road to Brown Station Road, which reduced the walk to a quarter of a mile. It also meant that we could see the bus coming and have plenty of time to run out and catch it. Before, when we were a mile-and-a-half off the main road, a few times we missed the bus and were late for school. Our father would take us to school in his older (antique) model car, which we would slouch down in the seats so our friends would not see us get out of the car when we arrive at the school.

During the 1960s, homes were not as close to each other as they are today. As children, we went into the wooded area behind our house to pick blackberries for my mother to cook a dessert called blackberry roly-poly. My mother cooked the blackberries, kneaded the dough until it was flat, then spread the blackberries on the dough and rolled up the blackberries inside the dough to cook inside the wood stove oven. I can still remember the wonderful aroma that filled our house. We did not think about the snakes or the thorny bushes; our only thought was getting to those blackberries for our mother. A few years later, a community of homes was built on Brown Station Road and the blackberry bushes were destroyed.

In the early years, the African-American families in the area were scattered by distance and lots of farm land. My early childhood friends consisted of my nieces, nephews, and cousins (Freda Staples' children) who lived about two miles away from us off Brown Station Road. Eventually, a few more African-American families, the Jacobs and Smalls, moved to Ritchie Marlboro Road. We spent time at one another's homes and went to school together.

My Parent's Discipline

"Foolishness is bound in the heart of a child; but the rod of correction shall drive it far from him." (Proverbs 22:15, KJV)

"Death and life are in the power of the tongue..." (Proverbs 18:21, KJV)

For many years, I addressed my siblings as ma'am or sir. We were taught as children that you address adults with manners and respect. You had to put a handle on an older person's name when addressing them and not say what, yeah, or just yes or no. Everything had to be done with proper respect toward your elders, no matter who they were. Finally, Melissa, the second oldest sister explained to me while I was in elementary school that I was her sister, and that I did not need to say "yes ma'am" or "no ma'am." By then it was difficult for me to stop because of being told to show manners to any adult. I still do it to this today.

My father and mother corrected us with harsh, negative words, a belt, or a switch, which is a branch from a tree limb. During the week, before we got inside plumbing and a full bathroom in our house, we bathe using a white metal basin. We took a full bath on weekends in a tin tub big enough to sit in. My mother often said that she was going to beat my siblings or me if we kept showing off, or that she owed us a beating—we never knew when it was coming. She would mentally pile up her punishments (mainly beatings on our behinds) until we got our Saturday night bath. After bathing, she would say as she prepared to beat us, "I owe you this from last week", or for the

21

period of the punishment whether a few weeks or days. Most of the time, I would have forgotten what I had done. I had let it go, but she did not. I always preferred to get my punishment right away. I knew it would hurt, but I got over it. The lingering promises of a beating hurt more than the actually beating. At times, when my mother had enough of our misbehaving, she reminded us that she owed us two, three or four beatings for what we had done. I remember being frightened because I never knew when she would make good on her promises.

My father, on the other hand, corrected us right away. I did not get as many beatings from my father as I did from my mother, but they would hurt just the same. My father's negative words were cutting to my soul. They hurt more than his spanking with his hand, switch, belt or whatever he had in his hands. We had welts on our bodies, but never permanent damage that was detrimental to our health but, our spirits were wounded. In those days, it was natural for parents to correct their children in such a manner. There was no one to report to about getting physical punishments in my era of the 1950s, 1960s, and 1970s. If we had the opportunity to report it, my parents would have been locked up on several occasions. Then again, none of us would have had the nerve to report them because such action was considered a natural part of rearing children.

My mother had a God-given gift to read your mind and discern what you were thinking as she was chastising you. It was as if she could hear the conversation in your mind and then tell you that you had better not say what you were thinking, or say aloud what you were mumbling under your breath. I tried hard not to do things to get a beating or get in trouble with either parent. Nevertheless, the dreaded beating would come every now and then. Both parents called us dumb, stupid or some other condescending words—I think it was natural in those days for some parents to talk like that to their children.

They thought it was a form of reverse psychology to make us do things that they knew would be for our own good.

My father often told me that I would not be anything because I ran my mouth too much and that eventually my mouth would get me into trouble. Because of what he said to me, I learned to be cautious about what I said for fear of saying the wrong thing, which I did at times and subsequently lead to verbal or physical repercussions. My parents were outspoken people. You seldom had to wonder what was on their mind. It is in my genes to be verbally expressive, yet I learned to quench what I wanted to say. However, at times I spoke before I thought about what I was getting ready to say and said it.

My mother helped us with our homework. She told me that I was dumb or stupid because I had a problem understanding concepts relating to certain subjects in school. Her motive was that she wanted to make sure that I got my education since she did not finish high school. My mom and I would sit beside the heated wood stove in the cold months to study my schoolwork. My parents felt this was the way to bring up their children so that we could have a better life than they had. My father dropped out of school in the sixth grade to help his father on the farm. Rachel, Melissa, and Joseph dropped out of high school, which our parents disapproved. Gregory was the first of my siblings to graduate from high school. We were treated the same despite the generational gap of the seven children. Our parents were stern with all of us especially about getting an education.

Sherita was smart and did very well in school. She could pick up concepts easily. She stuttered a lot, so it took her a long time to say what she had to say, so she did not talk much at home. I did enough talking on the phone with my friends for the both of us. If I did not understand something after a while, I would get frustrated and wanted to give up. I did not want to be called stupid or dumb so I hung in there until I understood. Looking back, I can see that both parents did not want me to be a quitter. Maybe this is what happened to them. They always wanted the best for us. And they gave to us the best that they could. We loved our parents.

Train up a Child

"Train up a child in the way he should go: and when he is old, he will not depart from it." (Proverbs 22:6, KJV)

I grew up during an era where children were seen and not heard—you were supposed to speak only when spoken to. The children left the room when adults were talking about things that they were not supposed to hear. I remember as a child that we had to leave the room when my sister Rachel brought adult-only records such as Moms Mabley and Richard Pryor when she and her children visited us. Unlike today's children, we would not dare engage in adult conversations.

Many children today are severely rude to their parents. That behavior would have never been tolerated in my parent's house. While growing up, whenever I raised my voice to express something to my mother or father out of frustration, I would be corrected quickly. By raising my voice above theirs, they thought that I was being rude, which sounded like I was sassing them. I soon learned, because my parents were thinking that I was fussing back at them, to keep my feelings locked inside of me. I feared being punished, let alone being embarrassed by either parent before my siblings. Because of a fear of repercussions from my parents, when I was upset with my father after being physically punished, I took my frustration out by cleaning my bedroom.

On beautiful days, I walked the long dirt road from my house on the farm to think and talk to God. Even though I was afraid of the horses or cows that could jump the fence and chase or hurt me, I walked anyway—walking and meditating for a long time before returning home. As the years passed, I continued to keep things locked inside of me instead of trying to resolve the issues or problems with the other party. I would share with people close to me who I knew would listen, but I realize now that I allowed a demon of fear in my life through my learned behavior of holding my verbal expressions back.

I remember in the summer lying on the hood of my father's car gazing into the sky. Sometimes, I could see a staircase leading up to heaven. When I saw the staircase, I thought about my maternal grandmother who died when I was two years old. I truly do not know why I thought of her every time I saw the stairs to heaven. I knew about God and heaven because my mother always took us to church on Sundays where we participated in youth activities. For the most part of my life, church was our primary outlet, outside of school, to engage with people outside our family.

My brother, Joseph brought his children, Gale and Kevin, to our house every day to go to school and in the summer. They stayed with us while he and his wife Jennifer went to work. One day, I got into an argument with Gale and Kevin about a game. They were three and four years younger than I. Gregory was the oldest of my siblings at home and thus in charge. They told Gregory about the argument over the game and for reason; he took a hot poking iron from the stove and branded me on one of my legs. I got so angry because he would not listen to my side of the story. So at the age of 12, I ran away from home for several hours.

I walked down the long roadway to Ritchie Marlboro Road with no plans of where to go. I met Raymond Jacobs, who lived on Ritchie Marlboro Road (Gregory's best friend) as I was walking. He gave me a ride to Joseph's house. I did not tell him that I had run away from home, but told him that I was going to my oldest brother's house that was about five miles from our house. Raymond let me out of the car at Joseph's mailbox, and I walked a quarter of a mile to his house. I do not know why I went to my brother's house; already I knew they would be at work. I guess I just wanted to tell on Gale and Kevin since I got in trouble because of them.

Shortly after arriving, and knocking on the door, I started the long walk back home, which helped to relieve the frustration inside me. This time I returned home on the back roads from Ritchie Marlboro Road, White House Road, and then Brown Station Road. Surprisingly, I told my mother what happened that day when she got home from work. She scolded all of us. I had a lot of anger and fear pent-up inside of me during my childhood. I was ready to fight, argue or throw something in frustration.

I know that my parents loved us because they always provided for us. I did not like my father yelling at me or saying negative and hurtful things about me. It was those belittling words that caused me as a little girl to remember the words of my father of how I would not be anything and that my mouth would get me into trouble. I would often cry or feel hurt because of those words. One day my mother came into the bedroom as I was crying and cleaning my bedroom out of frustration. She said I was crazy if I accepted what my father said, because she believed that since my siblings did not accept the negative things my father spoke, neither should I. All of us knew not to sass our parents and so it was best to listen and not dispute them.

My Self-Esteem Challenged by Sexual Abuse and Confusion

My father thought that I would be pregnant before I got out of high school—I was a virgin when I graduated from high school. Maybe his harsh words kept me in school and pure because my three older siblings did not finish high school and my two older sisters were pregnant before leaving school. My father did not want the pregnancy cycle to continue. My mom was pregnant with my oldest sister at age 17 by my father.

I remember in my 11th grade year that I had surgery for tonsillitis and had to stay at the hospital several days. I missed many days in the beginning of the school year. I learned from my mother a few years later that my father thought that I went into the hospital to have an abortion. I felt hurt and disappointed that my father thought that about me. I purposed in my heart that I would prove my father wrong, and determined that I would be somebody in life. I also decided then that my father would attend my high school graduation. This proved to be true when he attended my graduation, the first of his seven children that he attended. I was determined to prove the things that my father said and thought about me were wrong. I wanted my father to be proud of me and to say encouraging things to me. My father's words—good or bad—penetrated my inner being. I set out on a quest to be the greatest person that I could be and to achieve great things in life. I wanted my father to be proud of me and to dissolve the negative feelings about me.

My earlier years did not go without other challenges that caused me to further walk in fear. When I was nine years old, a male family member fondled me. I obeyed him because he was the adult. I was afraid to tell anyone because I did not want anyone to hate me. I felt guilt and shame. I was scared that I would be punished or that no one would believe me. I kept this secret to myself until I was in my thirties. I approached my relative about it after hearing a revivalist in the 1980s say that we must forgive others, even when they raped or molested you. Even though he denied the molestation had happened, because I confronted him, the burden lifted off me and the years of silence pent-up inside of me finally came out. I was free even though my relative was in denial—now it was between him and Jesus. I was in my forties, when I found out that the same male family member had molested other female family members. I continued to keep the pain on the inside rather than express it. I never told my mother or his wife. I wanted to keep the peace.

As a teenager at 15 years old, one of my father's best friends who lived with us propositioned me for sex. One Sunday evening I was home alone when he came back from one of his weekend drinking episodes. Since I shaved my father, he would ask me to shave him, which I did. This man asked me to have sex with him. I hurried to finish shaving him and left his presence. I shared this information with my mother and she immediately confronted the man. He apologized to my mother and it never happened again. I wondered even later in life why he selected me to do this wicked thing. Did I do something wrong? Surely, it must have been me. It caused me pain because as a child I wondered why he approached me like that since he was one of my father's best friends and like an uncle to us. I kept it on the inside and told no one except my mother. We never discussed it again. The secret was hidden for years.

Around age 17, I was on medication from our family doctor for a nervous stomach due to holding in my frustrations. The doctor told me if I kept it up that it would turn into an ulcer. I did not understand what an ulcer was, but it did not sound good. He gave me a prescription to help me. One weekend, I went to visit my sister Rachel who lived in Washington, D.C. Her daughter, Darlene, two years older than me, and I went out with three of her friends to a party in Glenarden, Maryland. We met three boys who wanted to take us to another party and we all piled into the car. They did not take us to another party but to a wooded area not far from the party and began to proposition us for sex. I began to pray and ask God to help us as my nervous stomach was reacting to the situation. Finally, they gave up and took us back to the party.

I thought I would be able to keep that secret inside because I did not want my parents or Rachel to stop me from visiting her in D.C. I loved going to parties to dance. The only other time I could have that kind of fun dancing was at Joseph and Jennifer's house when her family visited for social gatherings. Jennifer's brother, Jerome Hampton, was a man of the street who could dance. He taught me how to dance, as well as watching African-American dance programs on television, such as *Soul Train*. However, we had to tell Rachel because we came home so late in the morning. She was so upset with us for getting in a car with those boys. It was painful and the thought of being raped was too much for my nerves, but, I never told my parents, neither did Rachel.

Later, I was propositioned by one of my best friend's boyfriend. I was so hurt and felt betrayed by him. I felt guilty and blamed myself for allowing my girlfriend's boyfriend to take me home even though it was with her approval. I still felt it was my fault that he was in a position to proposition me. I did not understand what I did to cause this behavior or why he thought I would do such a thing with him against my best friend. I felt like dirt. What did I do? I was afraid of losing one of my best friends. I kept this secret inside of my heart, causing me more pent-up pain. It was approximately fifteen to twenty years later when I told my best friend. I felt relieved when I told her. She understood and was not upset with me especially since he was no longer in her life. I waited all of those years because I feared that she would not believe or listen to me as I was six years younger than her, still impressionable and enjoyed partying.

Again, I asked myself what did I do to cause that to happen? Why had those men singled me out for sexual favors? I felt maybe men only wanted me for sex. As a result of self-blame, I wondered if a male could love me for myself, and not just for my body. I hid the guilt of my past in my heart. Instead of dealing with it earlier in life, it followed me into my future. I learned that I had power in my body to get what I wanted from a man. But I praise the Lord for blessing me to commit (sell out) my life to Him by the age of 26. From ages 18 to 25, I had my experiences with men, partying, cabarets, bars, and other nighttime entertainment.

It was too bad that I felt that I was responsible for those events, when in reality I was not the guilty one. I realized later in life that I was not responsible for other people's behavior. I could not change those men that tried to hurt me sexually. Their behavior was not unusual in some of the African-American homes, but it was unusual for me and unacceptable behavior to me. Eventually, I learned to forgive them and let it go.

However, for years, the thought of possibly being raped lingered in my mind and I experienced fear when I found myself in few situations such as walking alone to or from my car or home. One day, in my thirties, I shared my fears of being raped with a friend, and that fear left me and it never returned.

The Rites of Passage

In 1970, my cousin, Laura Yates, who lived in Washington, D.C., started visiting me in Upper Marlboro and I visited her in Washington, D.C. Laura loved the country for the quietness, serenity, and fresh air; I enjoyed the city for the partying and the noise. Laura introduced me to some of her friends: Jeffrey "Jeff" Brown, Leon Mitchell, Andrew Lincoln and some others. Jeff was a very nice man who loved to sing. He was a large built man who was a cuddly, stuffed teddy bear at heart. Eventually Laura stopped going out with us to spend more time with her boyfriend. Jeff started to like me and came to Upper Marlboro to my house to take me and my best friend, Camille Johnson, and my niece, Gladys Snyder, to parties, clubbing, or just hanging out doing fun things. These men always treated me and my friends like ladies.

After graduating from high school in June 1972, at the age of 17, I started a federal government career with the federal government in Washington, D.C. I knew that my father would not want to stop his farm work to take me to the metro bus station about 15 miles away in Seat Pleasant, Maryland every day, and I did not have my driver's license at the time. If we wanted our father to take us some place, we had to tell him our appointment was an hour before so that we would be on time. I went to live with my brother Joseph and his family for about four months to have transportation to the metro bus station.

My childhood socialization (home, school, church, and friends) played a big part in influencing my adult personality and how I socialized with other adults. Because I did not deal with the stronghold of fear in my life from my childhood, I continued to hold back from expressing myself. At times, I still feared that I would elevate my tone and someone would get the wrong impression of me and misinterpret my intention. When I did not deal with the stronghold of "fear" it caused me to avoid confrontations of any sort to avoid losing relationships. I wanted to be accepted by everyone. I wanted to be successful at everything that I did. Failure was not an option.

Fear is "false emotions appearing real." At times I was afraid to take chances and other times, I did with confidence after pondering over the situation. Subconsciously, I could hear my father say that I would not be anything. Yet, I could hear my mother's voice within saying, "you can do anything you put your mind to do." Many times, I stepped out and took risks anyway, later to find that I had been successful. But fear continued to lead the way in my life for many years even in my relationships with men. I was afraid my relationships would fail because it would be like my parent's relationship who communicated at each other and not to each other. I failed to see the big picture for many years – they still loved each other, in the best way they knew how.

When I turned 18 years old, my mother told me that I was a woman and the weight of the world was now on my shoulders. At that moment, I truly felt the transfer of responsibility onto me as I experienced this rite of passage into adulthood.

It is amazing how our physical bodies can mature as it was created by God to do, but our inner person (our emotions) can remain in a child-like state, because of negative episodes or relationships in our lives. Unless we learn how to let go of the past, we will allow our past to influence our future. As for me, I carried some of those negative and hurtful words into my future, as I transferred my father as authority figure in my life, to other leadership figures in my life. Whereas, I felt the need to do things to please my father so that he would be proud of me, I later realized that I demonstrated the same behavior with other authority figures in my life, especially on my jobs. I realized that the bad habits that I carried from my childhood into my adulthood only caused grief in my life. I discovered that no matter how much I tried to please some of the bosses, they could never be pleased.

CHAPTER 2

THE LITTLE GIRL WITHIN CONTROLLING THE WOMAN OUTSIDE

My father was not the type of person who would readily give you money. If you asked for money, you had to listen to a lecture that "money doesn't grow on trees," that he "works every day," and that he "is not the bank." Normally when he gave us money, including my mother, he held the currency up to the light to make sure that he was not giving us more than he wanted to. My daddy, even with a sixth-grade education, was a financially savvy man.

My mother had to work for her own money in order to purchase the things that she wanted for herself. I had learned well, that if you wanted anything, you had better get it yourself. I learned to be independent from my parents. I was determined that I would make my own money so that I would not have to ask my father for anything or listen to him lecture. However, I did ask my father to help pay for me go to college after I had been working in the federal government for about two years. I realized quickly that it would take additional skills, or a college degree along with being a good employee, if I wanted to advance in my career. At the time, my father said that he did not have the money, since he was paying for Sherita to go to college. I believed my father and did not ask him again. At 18 or 19 years old, I asked my father to instead help me to buy a car so I would not have to depend on other people for transportation. Surprisingly, my father agreed to buy me a car, if, I bought a Volkswagen Beetle. I turned my nose up and said that I wanted a 1972 Chevrolet Nova. Since I did not get the car that he wanted me to have, I did not get any help from him. I should have listened to my father, because a year later the Maryland area experienced a gas shortage and long gasoline lines. If I had brought the Volkswagen Beetle, I would have spent less for gas during the gas shortage.

Because, I did not have a guaranteed means of transportation to get to the bus depot every day, I moved in with Joseph, my oldest brother and his family (wife, Jennifer and two children, Gale and Kevin). They lived about five miles from us in Upper Marlboro. Joseph and Jennifer worked in the Seat Pleasant area so they dropped me off every morning at the bus depot. I stayed with them for about four months. Then I moved to Marlow Heights with my niece, Darlene White, and her family. I stayed with them for about five months. Afterwards I moved to Landover, Maryland with my other brother, Gregory and his friends, Raymond and Jerome Jacobs (who are brothers) in their bachelor's apartment. I had it great because they were rarely home. I answered the phone and took messages. Gregory came home more than the others did. Since we went to school together and felt like family, the Jacobs brothers and I would tell people that we were cousins so that people would not get the wrong idea of having a woman in the apartment with three men. Later, their sister Dawn came to stay in the apartment for a while until she got married. We all got along. It was a wonderful arrangement.

The Jacobs lived within three miles of us in Upper Marlboro, Maryland. We spent time at each other's homes and went to school together. During this season of my life, I went to parties, cabarets, and socialized at the homes of my friends. I drank alcoholic beverages like wine and mixed drinks and thought "Is this all there is to this?," because as soon as I would get a buzz, it left as quickly when I went to the bathroom. I would never drink enough to get drunk because I always wanted to be in control of my senses and surroundings. I did not want anyone to take advantage of my friends nor me. Gregory let me use his Plymouth Duster when I needed transportation. I went to work every day and saved as much money as I could to buy my own car. I established a budget and learned to distinguish my needs from wants. I saved my money for a down payment for my own car in 1973. I tried hard to get my Chevrolet Nova, but I had to settle for a brand new 1973 Plymouth Duster. My first car, wow!

Gregory's son, Gregory Jr. (age 5) came to live with us in the apartment after I had been there for about a year. I made sure that he ate, bathed, did his homework, and I transported him to our sister Melissa's house every day for school. Gregory worked two jobs, but he came home at night while Gregory Jr. and I were sleeping. Our living arrangements were perfect since the men were not at home most of the time. Everyone always had some place to sleep. Gregory, his son and I kept the apartment for a while longer after the Jacobs brothers moved out of the apartment.

The Men in My Life

On my 19th birthday my close friend Jeff gave me my first surprise birthday party. At this party, I met a man name Teddy Gibson. Teddy and I started talking on the phone and then we went out for a date. On our first date, he stated that he did not want to take me home yet. He said that he wanted to spend more time with me and asked me to spend the night at a hotel with him. I told him that I had no plans to have sex with him. He told me that he just wanted to spend more time with me.

So we spent the night together, slept fully clothed and nothing happened. He did not try to have sex with me. He had gained my trust as a man who wanted me for more than my body. We spent the next three years in a dating relationship including living together in my apartment. He lavished me with clothes, shoes, money, and anything else that he deemed would make me happy. But, he was a lady's man. I knew that he could have any woman that he wanted yet, I knew that I did not want to share him intimately with anyone. Certainly I knew from his jealousy for me and that he did not want to share me intimately either with anyone else.

My life was good. I had a good federal government job, working on my college degree and a man who loved me. I was even attending church as well. I felt that I had everything going on. I knew that it was spiritually wrong for me to live with my boyfriend and not be married, but I allowed my love for him to overpower what I knew was the spiritually right thing to do. I remember thinking that I hoped he would not answer the phone if one of the church members called my home. Although, I could have said that it was my brother since he shared an apartment with my niece, Betty Snyder, and me. But I did not want to lie. My living arrangement was bad enough in the sight of God. I did not want to add being a liar to the spiritual charges.

One night I came home from a Friday night church service and he was waiting for me. I told him about the service and how the Lord dealt with me during the service. I told him that I could not have sex with him anymore because it was not right. I truly tried to stop having sex with him, but I loved him very much. I continued to go to church with this feeling that there was a change that took place in my life. I remember one of my nieces told me after the service that she did not think that I was saved. In essence, she felt whatever happened at the altar earlier that night was not an indication that I was saved and that Jesus had done a spiritual change in my heart. I did not understand my experience at the altar nor was it explained to me. I remember crying out loudly to Jesus to save me and to help me through my trials. Although I had this experience, I continued my relationship with my boyfriend, even though I knew it was wrong. At times, I questioned myself, whether my niece was right because I considered her more spiritually mature than I. Not having confidence in myself as a child caused me to lean on the opinions of others rather than trust my own opinion. I was afraid that I would make the wrong decisions.

When I joined the Bible Baptist Church in 1977, I enjoyed everything that I was assigned in the church such as teaching Sunday school to the youth, singing on the youth choir, and serving as a member of the nurses' auxiliary, as financial secretary, church secretary and youth director/coordinator. It was all fulfilling, along with my federal government job, my boyfriend, and attending college. Nevertheless, I knew that I could not stop myself from my living arrangement with Teddy without the help of the Lord. I loved him, but I would be convicted hearing the preached word, and then reading and studying the word of God for myself. Eventually, the Lord helped me to get it right by allowing circumstances to happen where my boyfriend and I finally broke up for good. God knew that I did not have the strength to do it alone, so He helped me.

Teddy had two beautiful little children. Some weekends they came to stay with us in my apartment. I met their mother, who did not seem to mind me in her children's life. I was told that the children would always come home talking about me. Teddy and I talked about marriage. I was afraid to make that type of commitment because I had a problem with his jealousy and mine for him. I did not trust in the area of fidelity. Although I knew that he loved me and I believed that I was his first love in his heart, but I was not the only sexual partner. Teddy and I had our ups and downs. Whenever he got angry with me, he would take back the clothes, coats, shoes and whatever else that he could get his hands on that he bought me, and take it out of my apartment to get back at me. Then I would call the police to get my things back and to have him removed from my apartment. On one occasion, I pressed charges and later wanted to drop the charges because Teddy and I had reconciled our relationship before we went to court, but the judge would not let me drop the charges.

Teddy threatened me on at least three occasions with a gun. He stated that if he could not have me then no one else would. Surprisingly, the stronghold of fear that I carried from my childhood did not affect me when he pointed the gun at me. I never showed any fear because I knew that would feed into his madness and obsession for me.

On the last occasion that he threatened me with his gun, I had gone to see him at the apartment that he shared with a woman he claimed was his sister. When I entered the apartment, the lady, his supposed sister, acted weird and said some strange things. Suddenly, Teddy came out of the bedroom with the teenage girl that I thought was his niece (her mother was supposed to be his sister). I was shocked; I discerned something inappropriate with the relationship. I left the apartment embarrassed and hurt and went to my car to go home. He came after me and tried to explain his behavior. I told him that I had to leave. Then he took out his gun to threaten me by telling me that he would hurt me. When he realized that the threat did not work, he then threatened to shoot one of the children playing outside. I told him that the children had nothing to do with us. He recanted his decision and allowed me to go home. I loved him so much that it was hard to let him go.

On another occasion, he tried to hurt himself with bug poison so that I would stay remain his girlfriend. He eventually drank some liquor and threw up the contents in his stomach. We tried to make our relationship work and during this time I never stopped going to church. I knew I could always find peace there. I asked God to take Teddy out of my life if he was not the man for me. I was tired of the roller-coaster relationship. I told God that I could not do it by myself because I loved him so much. God gave me the strength to let him go and to cut the soul ties, that deep emotional feeling in my soul, which continually drew me back to him. I knew that we loved each other and we were connected to one another by our emotions. I struggled with my emotions for him and said no when he wanted to see me, although he stated that he loved me and it was his fault for the troubled relationship. My body craved him because I loved him so much and wanted to be with him. I knew if we saw each other that we would be back together. I missed him and the nights without him were very difficult—I couldn't go to sleep at night because I was used to falling asleep in his arms. I cried myself to sleep every night for several weeks. I longed for him to hold me at night.

The loneliness was more than I could bear. But I knew that I had to take my hurt and move on. I had to let him go. The Lord had to help me through this one and He did. I prayed for strength to let go because I did not have the power or strength to do this by myself. I could not keep going through the love and pain roller coaster experiences in our relationship. I wanted to face my big hurt of letting him go for good and move on with my life. I had to find something else to do to keep my mind busy so that I would not dwell on my heart missing Teddy. Eventually, I moved on physically and emotionally. To help me let go of our past, I got more involved in church, work and college.

Later, I met Carlos West after I moved to another apartment complex. Carlos lived in the building across from my building in Landover, Maryland. We did not say more than hello to each other, probably because he did not know which of the three men was mine, since he would see Gregory's son, Gregory Jr., often with me.

One day, as Carlos was driving through my new neighborhood in Landover, Maryland he saw me and stopped. We talked. Finally, we started seeing each other. Even though I had not completely gotten over Teddy, Carlos and I started dating. We had wonderful times together going to parties, clubs, traveling, and enjoying each other. Initially, he did not want a commitment. He wanted things to stay as they were, but I wanted a committed relationship.

I was disappointed because I had fallen in love with him, and I did not want to be hurt again. I did not want to share him with another woman. It took me a while to get over the last man in my life. Carlos and I had our problems, but we continued to see each other. I knew that he loved me and I believed that he knew that I loved him. He was a wonderful man and fun to have in my life. I felt that he did not trust me, because he questioned me anytime I was a little late getting home. When he got angry with me, he would grit his teeth together; which would make me somewhat nervous, although I would try not to let him know it. Even though he never threatened me by saying that "no one could have me if he couldn't," I did not like the angry look on his face when he was upset with me.

Carlos was the type that would normally let things roll off his back. He was a laid-back person. If he got angry, then something truly happened to get him that way. We spent evenings either at my or his apartment, which was about a mile walking distance from my apartment. I enjoyed being with him. At times, he would go to church with me. I believed in my heart that this would be the man that I would marry and have his children. However, I was afraid of his temper and jealousy. I remember thinking that I could not live like that for the rest of my life, no matter how nice he was to me. He bought me wonderful gifts, we traveled to wonderful places, he took me on my first plane ride and I knew that he loved me and not because of the gifts he gave me. He never tried to discourage me from going to church. On Sundays, he even asked me if I was going to church. Eventually, I realized that I had to let Carlos go because we would compromise my relationship with Jesus by being sexually involved. Spiritually, I really wanted to live a committed life with the Lord, but physically, I enjoyed my sexual relationship with Carlos.

After several break-ups and getting back together, I decided that I did not want to continue the wave of pain in my life, so I broke up with Carolos once again. He decided he wanted the street life and I got busier with church, college and work. I wanted him so bad, but I could not share the street life with him if we got back together. I knew that I had to make a decision between him and God. Again, God won. I could always find the peace with God that I could not maintain in my relationships with men. I asked God to please take Carlos out of my life, if he was not the man for me. I loved him so much, and I did not have the will power to let him go by myself. God answered my prayers because He knew that I had a problem letting him go. A short time later when Carlos and I talked, he told me that it was not my fault that we broke up, and that he really loved me. My heart hurt so badly because I loved him. Again, I had trouble sleeping at night. The lonely nights without him beside me were too much many nights. It was so painful in my heart and I cried to be with him, but I knew that I had to make a choice and stick with it. He made me comfortable and I felt safe before his street life came into the picture. I did not want to accidentally get hurt because I was with him at the wrong place. I took my hurt and pain and moved on.

I had other men in my life in between the breakups because I did not want to be alone, but my heart would ache for the one I truly loved at the time. I enjoyed the attention of compliments, receiving gifts, money, and being treated like a lady. I felt spoiled and I enjoyed it. I often said that men should be glad that I was truly saved, because I knew that I could get what I wanted out of them. I did not have to sleep with all of these men; there was something that prompted them to want to give to me. But I did not want to use men because I did not want to be used myself.

We need to realize that some relationships are toxic and not healthy for us. I had to come to that conclusion so that I could move on with my life. As I previously stated, I could not do it without praying for the Lord to help me to let it go. Many times we stay in relationships that have been over for a while because we do not want to be alone. If we would let go of what is in our hands, then the Lord will eventually replace it with something better.

A New First-Place Man in My Life - Jesus

By the time I was 25 years old, my life took a turn. I decided that I wanted to be sold out to the Lord. I thought that if I died that I would go to hell for having sex outside of marriage and not paying my tithes. The Lord helped me with paying my tithes and I was so happy when I realized that God gave me 90 percent while He got the 10 percent. I was blessed going in and coming out. But, my flesh had a serious problem of wanting to continue to be sexually involved with the man in my life.

It sounds funny, but men helped me to get closer to Jesus. Whenever I was hurt in a relationship, I would get deeply involved in the church. I did things just to have Jesus proud of me. I was working out my soul's salvation through works. I wanted Jesus to be glad that I was His child and not disappointed in me, just like I wanted my earthly father to be proud of me for what I did. I believed that my heavenly father had to be appeased the same way. I learned later that God loves me unconditionally in spite of my shortcomings.

Throughout my life, I naturally analyzed things to have a better understanding of why something happened and especially to find out if I was the one to blame. I wanted to know what part I played in the altercation. I wanted to make corrections so that I could move on after admitting my faults and apologizing. After becoming a Management Analyst in the federal government in 1982, I learned more analytical techniques. This skill got me in trouble at times in my personal life because I wanted to analyze the things of God. Some things just happen and there is no analysis needed. But I sought for more reasons behind things that happened. I could not easily let it go. To let it go would mean that I might not find out why the trial happened in my life and what I was supposed to learn from it.

Because I walked in so much fear and anger in my childhood, the little girl remained a child and did not mature as an adult inside of me. I believe that because of my frustration when I could not express myself because of possible repercussions from my parents and other adults, I withheld my feelings inside. These hidden feelings followed me into my adult life. I tried to please people for some strange reason, by not trying to hurt their feelings whether they wronged me or not. I just wanted most people to like me. I feared that if they really knew me that they might not like me because they would see my faults and not accept me. I was afraid in heterosexual relationships that we would communicate with me like my parents — talking at each other instead of to each other for the 69 years and 9 months of their married life before my father's death. I failed to see the big picture – they still loved each other.

I experienced some awful times of pain and heartaches in my relationships. After each roller coaster experience, I took my hurt and moved on instead of waiting around for more pain. I continuously tried to make something work. After a period of time, I finally let it go because I knew that I had put in a lot of effort to make the relationship work. Still the little girl inside did not want to be hurt. She wanted to be accepted and praised. The little girl wanted to appease people to alleviate the feelings of disapproval. I realized that I was imposing this guilt and disapproval on myself — which I realize now was due to unresolved emotional issues of wanting to excel in everything I did. To mask any hurt during turbulent times in my life, I worked hard at everything: ministry, church, work and college; they became my life. I set out to be accomplished at everything that I did. I wanted everyone to speak well of me because my father told me to let other people praise me: *"Let another man praise thee, and not thine own mouth; a stranger, and not thine own lips"* (Proverbs 27:2, KJV).

The little girl inside continued to seek the approval of man. As an adult, many times in the workplace, no matter how much I did for my managers, it was not good enough. The problem that I experienced for years with fear of authoritative figures in my life was because I always tried to please my father. In actuality, I transferred the stern authority figure of my father to the supervisor or manager or the person in leadership in my life. I thought that I had to continue to please them in order to be accepted. Eventually, I learned the hard way to release people to think and behave the way they wanted to because I could not correct nor change anyone's mind.

If I knew that a person had a problem with me through their conversation with me or their behavior, I would hold it in for days or weeks and then confront them to try to resolve the matter. After a period of time, people tended to forget what the grievous problem was about. When I talked to them trying to resolve what I thought was a problem, they asked me what I was talking about, or that they had no problem with me. After being told that everything was okay between the person and me, I still felt a bit of tension, but continued to question myself to find out what I did wrong. I could fix me, but I could not fix anyone else even after apologizing. I had to learn to let it go. It was hard because I wanted to be in harmony with that person.

It took me years to learn to stop taking on other people's problems and their opinions of me. I could not fix their attitude towards me nor should I have thought that I could. I finally had to learn how to love myself more than any other human being. I know it sounds strange, but as long as I showed low self-esteem then people walked on me and thought nothing about hurting my feelings. I taught them indirectly how to treat me by my passivity in many situations and a non-confrontational approach. Finally, I learned to love me and see myself the way Jesus sees me and loves me. I stopped analyzing other people's behavior and let it go. My attitude became, if you like me, you do, and if you don't, it's okay with me—let us move on. The little girl finally grew up to allow the woman to make the decisions.

The Girl Grows Up

I have experienced many challenges in my personal, professional, and spiritual life over the past few years. At times, I wondered emotionally if I would make it. However, Jesus brought me through it all. I had to experience the pain and I had to let the pain from the challenging trials go. I had to learn to allow the Bible to take root in specific areas that I was being defeated. In other words, I had to trust in God's Word that He would cause me to victorious. I had to take the negative and make it positive. I had to learn to forgive in order to move on spiritually. I learned that one can move on physically, but spiritually and emotionally, you are still at home base in the game of life. I had to let it go. It was difficult because I wanted to be in harmony with everyone, even though the Bible speaks of being careful when everyone speaks well of you.

The Holy Spirit would minister to me to let go of the past to embrace the new. Letting it go meant the little girl inside had to give way to maturity, thus releasing the woman in me to be in charge, to move on in the situation. I will not forget what happened because I am human. If someone asks me in five or ten years about an incident, I will probably not have amnesia and say I forgot. This could be a set-up for a repeat performance, which I don't want. Fortunately, I will recall past incidents without the intensity of the hurt and pain they once had in my life. The pain and hurt have helped to launch me into spiritual maturity, and taught me to love myself and to build healthy self-esteem so that I will fulfill God's purpose in my life.

Letting it go is facing up to the reality that something bad happened to me, but, I was willing to release it into the hands of God for the healing of my broken heart, soul and spirit. In other words, I had to forgive. It is a heartfelt decision to release the people who hurt me from the obligations incurred when they mistreated me. God showed me that I had to forgive my brethren "seventy times seven." Even now, I still experience times when it is challenging to forgive, but the Holy Spirit quickens me to let it go. I wish that I could tell you that it's easy, but it's not. Our flesh often rises up to take revenge.

Letting go is more for me than for the other person. I need to forgive to move on in my spiritual and physical life. For me, letting go meant that I allowed the little girl in me to digress, to allow the woman to handle the trials in my life. The girl handles situations in an impromptu manner and pouts in frustration and emotional pain. Yet, the woman takes authority and handles the situation appropriately and straight-forward, thus being an overcomer and not repeating the trial again. The woman within lets it go. She has learned from life that you chalk the good and the bad up to experience and move on.

It took me a long time to realize that as long as I allowed the little girl inside to control the woman outside, I was delaying my destiny. In releasing the hurt and pain, I was able to move forward. God has great things for all of His children. But I could not get everything that God has for me until I understood what it meant to allow the Lord to bring me into spiritual maturity. And, I need to be in position to receive what God has for me. I have learned to walk in authority, to be an overcomer, and not repeat some of the same trials.

Around the age of 26, I realized that my father had tried to use reverse psychology on me to make me determined to make it—which worked. It could have been a self-fulfilling prophecy if I became what he said about me. I wish that he had used a different approach because I went into overdrive as an achiever and I could not stop myself. I felt that I had to prove to him that he was wrong regarding the negative things that he said about me. Finally, at age 37, while on a cruise with my mother, father, and sister Sherita, I asked daddy why was he so hard on me growing up. He said he saw something in me. I said to him, "You could have thought of a different approach." The harsh spoken words, even from loving parents caused emotional pain in my life that led to relationship issues in adulthood. I had to be careful to strike a balance between being determined, and being an overachiever for the wrong reasons.

All that I went through in life, good or bad, helped to make me who I am. God used my trials to make me stronger for the next trial and to encourage other people. If you do not deal with the little girl on the inside, no manner of cosmetic make-up will stop the little girl from controlling the woman. Sometimes, to gain respect, women try to look mature and beautiful on the outside, rather than becoming Christ-like in character and allowing the Lord to make the transformation in their life.

"I beseech you therefore, brethren by the mercies of God, that you present your bodies a living sacrifice, holy, acceptable unto God, which is our reasonable service." (Romans 12:1, KJV)

It is not unscriptural for a woman to want to be attractive. True beauty, however, begins within a person—inside out. A gentle, modest, humble, and loving character gives a light to the face that cannot be duplicated by the best cosmetics and jewelry on any woman. Women who are not walking in the fullness of God's greatness for their lives will wear a mask to hide the true person. There is a time and a place for the little girl to play, i.e., in your marriage to keep it interesting when the little boy in the man wants to play. But, the true change in our lives grows as we spend time in the Bible, allowing the outward woman to change from the inside out.

CHAPTER 3

THE CALL TO MINISTRY

"Then the word of the LORD came unto me, saying. Before I formed thee in the belly I knew thee; and before thou camest forth out of the womb I sanctified thee, and I ordained thee a prophet unto the nations. Then said I, Ah, Lord God! behold, I cannot speak: for I am a child. But the LORD said unto me, Say not, I am a child: for thou shalt go to all that I shall send thee, and whatsoever I command thee thou shalt speak. Be not afraid of their faces: for I am with thee to deliver thee, saith the LORD."

Jeremiah 1:4-8, KJV

I have been in church all my life. My mother took us to church every Sunday that she could get my father or Joseph to take us. My first church was a Methodist Church in Upper Marlboro, Maryland, until the age of seven. In the Methodist Church, I participated in church programs, in plays, and singing in the choir. I remember my father gave us about 15 cents for church. I kept a dime and put five cents in the offering plate. After church, we would convince my mother to ask Joseph to stop by a country store called Ritchie so we could get some candy, a cupcake or a soda before going home.

After several years in the first church, my mother took us to join a Baptist church in Forestville, Maryland. I participated in church programs singing in the choir, doing plays, and other things, which I enjoyed. I accepted Christ into my life and was baptized around 12 years of age. I remember my first communion and feeling good because I was now like the others who could take communion.

My mother took us to another Baptist Church in Washington, D.C. a couple years later. Again, I participated in the church programs. About the age of 18, I planned my first solo church program. I invited a local guest choir to perform at the evening service as a fundraiser. It gave me the confidence that I could do the same type of event again, if I had to.

As the years progressed, I got to a place where I wanted more from God. I certainly did not realize at the time that I would be called into the ministry. In 1977, I prayed to God to send me to a church where I had something to do. I told Him, if I did not have anything to do in church, I would make excuses why I should stay in bed on Sunday mornings. God answered my prayers. One Sunday, I visited the Bible Baptist Church in Washington, D.C. The pastor's preaching style reminded me of Dr. Martin Luther King, Jr. I enjoyed the preaching so much that I was ready to join the church during my first visit.

Serving in the Church

On my third visit, I joined the Bible Baptist Church. Immediately, Deacon Howard Godwin, the chairperson of the deacon board asked me to teach Sunday school. I studied every weekend to prepare for my Sunday school class. I taught Sunday school to children ranging from ages 2 to 18, and the Lord taught me how to keep the attention of everyone in my class. Then Trustee Charles Pope, chairperson of the trustee board asked me to type the financial report—another blessing from God. Now my life consisted of going to church, work, college and going out with friends on some weekends. I was so happy because I felt needed and wanted. I had my own job so I did not have to depend on anyone to give me money; I went to college and paid for it myself. I went out on weekends because I enjoyed being with my friends and dancing. I had my church where I was needed and I grew tremendously.

I eventually became the youth leader for our church. Every fifth Sunday was Youth Sunday. When I asked the youth to participate in the service, they did it. I was very proud of all of them. I loved them and they loved me. I praised them and encouraged their parents to do the same. I shared the story of my father's negative and hurtful words spoken into my life. However, I was determined to prove my father wrong.

I know now how careful parents must be with what is spoken, because not all children are as zealous as I was to prove my father wrong. Some self-fulfilled prophecies that parents speak over their children come to pass, whether they realize it or not. This is why we must take heed to what we say about our youth, and realize that our words have the ability to produce life or death.

The children became so dear to me and I wanted them to have exposure to positive influences, so I planned bus trips to museums, amusement parks, and other places of interest. We were good to each other and for each other. In jest, I remember the pastor said one Sunday that parents have to be careful with Sister Harrison because she can steal their children. In truth, I simply showed them respect and they did likewise to me.

One Sunday evening in January 1983, following a youth-sponsored program, I developed a terrible headache by the time I reached home. I could not understand where the pain came from because I had such a wonderful time at church. I called one of my friends at the church, Marjorie Newton, and explained my plight. Before she arrived at my house, I cried out to the Lord to heal me. The only relief that I got was when I placed my head in the opened Bible—the pain stopped, only to start again when I took my head out of the Bible. When my friend arrived, I explained to her again what was happening to me. As she anointed me with oil and prayed, I had my eyes closed and saw a vision of Jesus with a thorned wreath around his head. The blood from his brow was streaming down his face onto my hands to wash them. I felt cleansed. I heard Him say, "feed my sheep." I heard it again a second time. I did not understand what He meant and pondered the saying in my heart for several months. The vision was so real to me. I was healed that night of the headache.

One night at Bible study, the pastor briefly talked about dreams and visions. As the words formed in my mouth to share my vision with the people, the first lady spoke and shared a dream that she had and how her husband did not believe her. So, I did not share my vision since I did not know what to make of it. I kept it in my heart and pondered over it from time to time.

After the experience in January, the Lord filled me with the Holy Ghost with evidence of speaking in tongues. One night at the altar, He told me that He would take me down to nothing, but He would bring me back. I did not understand what He meant until much later. Due to a misunderstanding in the church, I was taken down from being church secretary, financial secretary, Sunday school teacher, and everything else that I enjoyed doing. I was so hurt that I cried when the pastor called me to say that he was putting someone else in most of those positions. I called Deacon Godwin, the chairperson of the deacon board, who talked with the pastor on my behalf since I was single.

I believe the misunderstanding started when I volunteered to do the financial records before I started back to college. Even though I knew my schedule would be challenging, the other church member who usually did the task was not available. Later, when she was available, I was not available because of my evening college classes. I could not understand what I had done except that I said I was not available to do the financial documents (documenting the member's tithes and offerings from the envelopes to another document for church record and income tax purposes). After this incident, other situations began to surface in the church that did not directly relate to me but my name was involved in. I talked with my sister Melissa who was an evangelist in another church. She agreed that I should talk to the pastor and leave the church.

Moving On

So, in July 1983, the Lord led me to leave the church. I told the pastor that I came to be a blessing and not to hurt anyone. It was time for me to leave. He told me that he had taken away my duties, but he did not intend for me to leave. I left the church and started attending other churches until I joined Capital Church of Christ, a Pentecostal church. My Pentecostal experience started to unfold more here, although it had started in the Baptist church earlier that year. I began to speak in tongues more and experienced other manifestations of the Holy Spirit in my life. I experienced such a tremendous outpouring of God's anointing on my life. At times, I could not stand under the anointing, collapsing under the unction of the Holy Spirit. The Lord started the call on my life while in that Baptist church, but now in Capital Church of Christ, He made the calling on life clearer.

In November 1983, while visiting my nephew Sylvester Snyder (who is a minister), in New Jersey, my mother and I visited the church he attended. It was there that the Lord furthered the call on my life that He started in the Baptist church. While at my nephew's church, I went to the altar to pray and seek understanding about the hurts that I had experienced at my previous church. I also wondered why my old boyfriend Carlos had reappeared in my life, rekindling the fire in my heart for him. While in prayer, the awesome power and presence of the Holy Spirit caused me to fall down to the floor. I felt like I could not move nor wanted to move, but just listen to what the Holy Spirit was saying to me. The Lord told me that He had to do that to me because it was the only way He could get my attention, since I was so busy doing so many things (I had the Martha syndrome). I stayed on the floor under the anointing for what seemed like a long time. The Holy Spirit began talking with me and told me to heal the sick, raise the dead and cast out demons in Jesus' name. He also told me to go to school, and which two pastors to share what He had told me. At the time, I was working on my Associate Degree in Business Management. Later, I realize that the Lord wanted me to go Bible College to learn more about Him along with my Bible Study.

Soon after returning home I was obedient and talked with both pastors. I shared with my current pastor, Pastor Thomas Logan and another pastor, Pastor Julia Jenkins, who left Bible Baptist Church the year before me to start her own church. Pastor Jenkins knew me quite well and was familiar with the duties I was responsible for at the church. One night I shared my vision with Pastor Logan prior to a prayer service. He asked me if I had planned to stay, which I did. Later in the service, he shared with the church what God told me to share with him. He called me to the front of the church, where he and several elders prayed and laid hands on me for the impartation of the gifts of the Holy Spirit into my life. Although I worshipped in Baptist Churches for several years, I was familiar with the Pentecostal experience of laying on of hands as spoken of in Acts Chapters 6 and 8.

Whom they set before the apostles: and when they had prayed, they laid their hands on them. And the Word of God increased; and the number of the disciples multiplied in Jerusalem greatly; and a great company of the priests were obedient to the faith. And Stephen full of faith and power, did great wonders, and miracles among the people. (Acts 6:6-8, KJV)

Then laid they their hands on them, and they received the Holy Ghost. (Acts 8:1, KJV)

I stayed at this church for several months trying to find my place in ministry. When the Lord said to me, "Go ye," I told the pastor. He asked if I wanted to start a home Bible study. I told him that it would take much faith and I was afraid because I did not know what to do. He said that he would get me started. He asked if I was married. I said no, and then he replied that I would get married. This was confirmation that I knew that the Lord would bless me one day with a husband. While waiting on more guidance from my pastor, because I did not want to pressure him and seem too anxious, I signed up to be a Sunday school teacher. A position was not available so I assisted a friend whenever she needed me in her Sunday school class. I truly missed being active in church other than participating in the offering and the worship service. I went to church, work and college. I again heard the Lord say "Go." I shared it with the pastor and then I left the church in July 1984. I wondered where to go. I liked being a part of a church family, but I knew that God led me to leave. I was obedient to the Lord.

I visited Pastor Julia Jenkins of Hope Mission Church with whom the Lord told me to share my experience. We talked again about my vision in January 1983 while in New Jersey visiting my nephew. I told her that the Lord was leading me to come to her church, but I did not know how long I would be there. In July 1984, I joined Pastor Julia Jenkins' church. Shortly after being there, she told me I would preach my initial sermon (in September 1984.) I was frightened by the responsibility. One day while on a bus trip returning to the church, I was suddenly compelled to write what the Holy Spirit gave me. It was the first message that I preached in September 1984. The title was "Jesus Is Looking for Disciples" and my reference scripture was John 1:43-51.

At Hope Mission Church, I was a Sunday school teacher, Evangelist, chairperson of the trustee board, fund raiser, and assisted the Pastor coordinating retreats. I also taught home Bible studies to an older lady that I met on one of my ministry engagements, and later to Jocelyn Whitfield, a co-worker and her three children. I did this under the approval of the pastor. I stopped when God said to stop, which was a year later. I received my Christian Worker's license from the Assemblies of God organization in February 1987. The Lord blessed and continued to use me to be a blessing in whatever capacity that He needed me.

After three and a half years, I heard the Lord say that it was time to prepare to leave soon. I thought, "Why now?" since I loved the pastors and my church family. I did not want to leave my familiar surroundings. I cried to God several times, and I made excuses why I needed to stay a little while longer. I was also afraid of what the pastor would say about my leaving as I did not want to be belittled nor made to feel like I did not hear from God. Never an impulsive person, ninety-five percent of the time I thought about situations in my heart and mind over and over again before making a decision. I visited another church one Sunday morning, and it seemed like the message was meant just for me. No one knew what I was going through but Jesus. I prayed for the Holy Spirit to help me to talk to her. That night I called my pastor to tell her what the Lord told me. She did not agree that it was time for me to leave. I knew her and her husband loved me as a spiritual daughter and I looked to them as my spiritual parents and leaders of my church—that was why it was so hard to leave them.

In our conversation, I told Pastor Jenkins that if I missed God, I would come back. No matter whether I agreed with any of my pastors or not, I did not get into an argument nor disrespect them. I was taught as a child that you respect ministers. I always said, "God you put that person here, so fix it," and He did in His timing and His way.

While in transition, I visited other churches to see where God would lead me to be a member. I shared with one pastor friend who told me that God said that I should be at her church. I got upset with God because I felt that He did not tell me first. Finally, I realized that if He wanted me to know something that He would tell me. I did not join her church, but waited on God for direction. Early spring of 1987, I attended Calvary Church of Christ, a church where a close evangelist friend, Glenda Bailey attended. Pastor Jerome and co-pastor Edna Long invited me to join their ministers at their home for one of their monthly all-night prayer fellowships. In the morning, the pastors prepared breakfast for everyone before the ministers left to go home. I questioned if I truly heard from God to join that church since there were approximately 12 ministers on staff already. I said to God, "You know that I love to work in the church, what am I going to do here?" I was obedient and I stayed. A few weeks later, the pastor asked me to be the director over the new believers and new members, to minister to them at the altar, and to teach a separate Bible study to this group.

New Challenges

Again, I was faced with how to do something I had never done. I did not have a clue about how to start a Bible study class of new believers in a church setting. I prayed for God's guidance. The pastor prepared a one-page outline which afforded me the opportunity to research the subject more thoroughly. I was nervous; however, the class grew spiritually by leaps and bounds. Every Monday night, I went to the church to teach, giving out lessons and tests, and homework. My goal was to help people fall in love with God's Word. I felt so privileged by Jesus to be chosen to teach this class.

I was always a high-energy type of person, so I gave my all in class. When I went home, I collapsed from being tired, but happy to be used by the Lord. I was still working everyday and going to college at night. I just wanted to please Jesus. Finally, Pastor Long left the lesson planning up to me. Although I still experienced challenges in my life, I was happy and fulfilled. In time, I became a trustee and taught at the church's annual retreats. Pastors Jerome and Edna Long licensed me in October 1988.

The Lord led me to coordinate a minister's retreat held at a retreat house several hours away in Pennsylvania. Both pastors and several of the ministers went and all were blessed. At the retreat, the Lord dealt with me severely that it was time to leave Calvary Church of Christ. I cried and felt the pain of leaving my pastors and church family, and the responsibilities that I enjoyed. The Sunday that all of the ministers got back from the retreat was to be my last Sunday at the church. I kept asking God to let me stay. That morning I cried through the whole service because God kept telling me that it was time to leave. I put out a fleece, asking God to allow the pastor to be available in his office after church where no one would inter-rupt us until I finished talking with him. God did just that. It was a miracle because it seemed every Sunday several people wanted to talk with the pastor after service. When I told the pastor I was leaving, he said that he did not want me to leave. Finally, he said something that I would never forget when he told me he would leave the porch light on for me. I felt that he meant that whenever I wanted to come back I was welcome. The light represented me finding my way back to the church. It was so beautiful.

At the time, I felt that God was leading me sometime in the near future to start a church, something I did not want to do because I was afraid of the responsibility. That Sunday evening, my sister Melissa, who had started a church a year earlier, called to say that some of her children who attended the church said that I had been crying through the whole service. I explained to her how the Lord told me that it was time for me to go. She asked me to come to help with her new church until the Lord showed me what to do. I agreed since she is my sister, and I knew that I would be used at her church.

While at my sister Melissa's (Pastor Snyder) church, Salvation Christian Center, I served as an evangelist, taught beginners Bible study, and assisted with the business of the church as needed. I taught seminars and held one-day conferences. I stayed about three years. While I was helping my sister, the beginners Bible study class grew. We started out in her son's home across the street from the church since we did not have room in the church (a storefront church at the time). My nephew's wife was at home, but for a personal reason initially she did not join us. After several weeks, she joined us in her home for Bible Study. She was so enthused with the Word of God that she stated that she went to work studying the lesson plans that I gave the students. Also, she shared the lessons over the phone with her sister and other people. I was honored that God used me to reach people with His Word.

Pastor Snyder ordained me in March 1992 after telling me that it should have happened before then. I was told that now I could marry and bury folks. I was not pressed about doing either one, but to my surprise, I conducted my first wedding in May 1992. I got a phone call from Pastor Snyder early one morning before going to work to say that I would have to perform a wedding because of a change in the plans of the other pastor scheduled to do it and so she and her husband could be a part of the ceremony like the other parents. The Holy Spirit gave me the wedding vows for the couple, which was my niece Carrie and her fiancé, Billy. I had one week to prepare for the wedding. I met with the couple to show them the draft wedding vows, which they accepted. Since people were not aware of the change in who was officiating the wedding, they were surprised when I came out of the waiting area to start the ceremony. The marriage ceremony was so anointed. I received compliments from a lot of people, especially pastors in attendance. I especially felt honored and blessed when one particular pastor, Joshua Mills, told me that he was blessed by the wedding vows and the ceremony. I held him in high esteem because he was a respected leader in the clergy and church community.

In August 1994, I conducted my second wedding, which was for my nephew, Melvin and his fiancée, Darlene Curry. They asked me to write the wedding vows and once again the Holy Spirit gave me vows tailored to the couple. After receiving so many compliments about the wedding vows, I decided to have them copyrighted. Since it was the pastor's children getting married, again she asked me to perform the wedding so that she and her husband could be a part of the ceremony like other parents. I was honored to be asked to do this. Yet, I was so nervous. I thank God for how He equips us to do things and we can only say that it is the Lord, and He gets all the glory.

Elder Larry Joyner

In 1992, Elder Larry Joyner joined Salvation Christian Church. He had been in another church with my sister and her children before she became a pastor. He was like a son to Melissa and a sibling to her children. He spent time at her house with her family. She had ministered to him and his first wife as they went through marital challenges. I remember my reaction when he shared with me at Melissa's church that he had gotten a divorce. I thought to myself, "Why are you telling me? I cannot judge you." I told him that I hoped everything would work out for him.

At the time, the Lord had been dealing with me about leaving the church. I kept it to myself for over a year. Again, I did not want to leave and be in-between churches, learning new people, and proving myself all over again. I loved my pastor/sister, and church family and my responsibilities. I talked with my sister about the Lord leading me to leave the church. She was disappointed and told me that she understood how the other pastors felt when I shared with them that I was leaving their churches. To my amazement, she told me that I would have to tell the church. So, one Bible study night I made the announcement to the church. Some cried and some asked where I was going. All I could say was that the Lord told me that it was time to leave the church. I felt like Abraham going into a far country not really knowing where he was going to make his home until God showed it to him.

I left Salvation Christian Center in September 1993 and for about a year and a half I continued to pay my tithes and support the church when I could. I wanted to hear clearly what God wanted me to do. God told me to go to Continental Seminary in Florida. I enrolled in their correspondence program for the Ph.D. degree in December 1993. I tried to make it work, but I would get writer's block. I did not have the confidence in myself that I could discipline myself to stay focused on completing the correspondence program. I started work on my Ph.D. at Hallelujah Christian Bible College in February 1994. The funny thing is that the Ph.D. program at the local Bible College also required me to write many papers.

The course work at Hallelujah Christian Bible College was very challenging and mind boggling, but I did not allow it to defeat me. I persevered until I got it all done and made a B average in the program. However, during the Hallelujah Christian Bible College program I burned out physically, mentally, emotionally, and spiritually. It was challenging to hear from God in this state. I went to classes year round, including the summer. I felt that my brain was on overload with working a full time job, and working on two Ph.D. programs—Hallelujah Christian College regularly and Continental Seminary inconsistently. I wanted to get it over with and to enjoy life, but I was also glad to be busy because it eliminated me thinking about things that were not productive to my spiritual well-being. To complete my schooling, I took out a loan from my credit union to pay for the Ph.D. coursework in full, thus saving money with an early payoff plan.

During this period of time, the Holy Spirit showed me that it was not His perfect will for me to go attend Hallelujah Christian Bible College. I felt that I was better in a classroom setting than trying to be disciplined enough to complete a correspondence program. I had done well in my classes, except for statistics which I had to repeat before finally making a B grade with the help of a tutor. The tutor helped me to understand the concepts of statistics.

One day, around 1995, while in prayer, the Holy Spirit said that Hallelujah Christian Bible College would be closed before I was finished paying the loan. He was right. The college closed due to personnel and administrative reasons. I cried because I had finished my last course when that happened in September 1997. I had paid off the program in full and now my money was gone. Every school I called told me that they were sorry about what happened, but I had to take their courses at the Ph.D. level. God gave me favor with Continental Seminary and they accepted only three classes for their program. I appreciated the favor, but I still was not halfway finished with Continental Seminary. It had taken me a long time to complete their correspondence courses because I focused on classes at Hallelujah Christian Bible College.

I talked with Melissa regularly since I always believed in a spiritual covering. After one a half years, she told me to come back to the church until the Lord showed me where to go. I had a large beautiful home with many rooms, yet, I went to a hotel to hear from God. God told me that He took me out of Egypt and for me not to go back. I believe God wanted me to see that it takes faith to move from my comfort zone to a place where He was trying to take me. (Genesis 12:1, "Now the Lord said unto Abram, Get thee out of thy country, and from thy kindred, and from thy father's house, unto a land that I will show thee:") But I begged God because I did not want to be out of a local church—I did not like being alone. I did not mind being under the leadership of someone else because I did not have to be responsible for the ultimate operation of the church.

Larry and I started dating each other as friends in April 1994. Later our friendship grew to the point that he hinted about marriage. I felt that it was alright to date him, but not to talk about getting married, because of the relationship that he had with my sister and her children, he felt like a family member more than a romantic interest. Besides we went to the same church and he was younger than I, and I personally did not care for either. Since it was MY policy, I could change it, so I dropped the policy and proceeded to date him for the next two years.

Many times, we implement standards in our lives based upon what we believe we will or will not do. Sometimes we will lower our standards because we believe that a person or thing is good for us. It is wise to allow a person or thing to measure up to our standards, instead of lowering our standards to the person, to get what we think is good for us.

One night in April 1996, our guest revivalist, Pastor Scott Madison, was staying in my home with his wife and daughter. He told Larry and me that God showed him that we were soul mates. I cried because I never wanted Larry as more than a good friend. But did God want something more? I had also rejected the idea about us being more than friends because I felt God said he was not the one. I did not feel we were soul mates, although I really liked Larry and I had fun with him while dating, since we could talk about anything. When he saw me stressed or burnt out from work or my college workload, he would take me out for a ride to a place of my choice to give me a break. We would spend the whole day together and I would feel better and have more energy to continue on in my Ph.D. studies. God still mandated that I finish Continental Seminary, so, in obedience, I continued from 1993 to 2004 when I finished.

Graduations

Over a short period of years there were many events that caused me an emotional overload. In July 2003, my father got very sick and had to go to a rehabilitation home to learn to use his motor skills again before he returned home in August 2003. In December 2003 he suddenly got sick while in the hospital and he passed away, even though we thought he would get better and eventually return home. I was so hurt about my father's death. I saw him earlier that night, and encouraged him to eat so he could get his strength back and come home.

In October 2003, we found out that Sherita had colon cancer. Sherita and I were always close and took our vacations together. But we got closer as we prayed every Saturday morning for several months until she went into the hospital in June 2004. Sherita was in the hospital when I went to Continental Seminary in Florida for my graduation (June 2004). She was always there to join my celebrations in life – but not this time.

My divorce became final on July 13, 2004. Sherita passed on July 29, 2004. I did not think that I could face another battle. I needed strength from the Lord. I felt that I needed and wanted a man in my life that would hold me until I felt assured that I could make it through another trial. I got my spiritual nourishment from the Lord, but I wanted the help from the right human being.

In June 2004, prior to the graduation ceremony, my academic advisor told me that I had a great dissertation, and that he could see that I had put a lot of work into it, and it was well written; however, I omitted the footnotes in my dissertation. He stated I could still graduate, but I had to resubmit the dissertation with the footnotes before I could get the degree. He also suggested that I should publish the dissertation as a book because the content could help all races and not just African Americans. Immediately, I added the footnotes to my dissertation and over-night express-mailed it back to the seminary before I flew to

Florida for the graduation. Two weeks after the graduation, I called to discover that the seminary had received my revised dissertation, but they had not read it with the inclusion of the footnotes. I was informed that I would hear from them after they completed their review. When I did not hear from them after a couple of months, I decided to reread my dissertation. Instead of letting go of the dissertation, I read over the dissertation thinking that there must be something else wrong with the paper since I had not heard anything. I continued revising the research paper to make it better. I should have left it alone until I heard something from the college. Finally, in December 2004, I contacted the school to say that I had mailed the revision to my dissertation that I submitted in June 2004. My academic advisor said that he could not re-read the revised dissertation until he returned to the college after the holidays. At that time, I called him back to find out the status of my research paper. He asked me why I had resubmitted another revised dissertation and asked me if I had gotten a green document that told me the dissertation had been accepted. I said no. My academic advisor apologized. He reiterated that he could tell that I put a lot of work into the document. He stated it was a very good document on marriage that could help African-Americans and any other race. He stated that I was not required to defend my dissertation before a board since I enrolled into the school before that procedure became effective. He said that he was still interested in talking with me about my paper and I agreed to talk with him. Various things happened in my life over the next couple of months, so it was March 2005 by the time I talked with him about my dissertation. I asked if my degree would be dated June 2004. He stated no since we had our conversation after the graduation date and it was a Florida law that it could not be backdated. I was so disappointed, but relieved that I had finally done what God wanted me to do.

CHAPTER 4

THE MARRIAGE

"And said, For this cause shall a man leave father and mother, and shall cleave unto his wife: and they twain shall be one flesh? Wherefore they are no more twain, but one flesh. What therefore God hath joined together, let not man put asunder." (Matthew 19:5-6, KJV)

I abstained from sex for about 17 years leading up to the day that I got married for the first time at age 42. I was sold out to the Lord in every area of my life, so I kept my word to the Lord to honor Him with my body. I wanted my wedding night to be special to me and the man that I married.

Like everything else in my life, I desired to excel in my marriage. I had my desire list for a mate– someone I could talk to as a best friend, a man devoted to God and filled with the Holy Spirit, who would love me as Christ commanded in His Word, to be the spiritual head of our home, educated, financially prepared, good credit, and matched my salary and property assets. Oh yes, I had my desire list. But a lot of things I gave up on because I did not see them as important any longer because I loved Larry for who he was and not for what he possessed. I believed that what was not fulfilled on the desire list, over time we could accomplished those things together by complimenting one another. I realized that you cannot make a person change; they must want to change on their own. I did not go into the marriage thinking I would change this man, based on the known flaws, once we were married. I knew that I also had some thorns on my rose bush, and that meant to me we were both not perfect, yet we could complement one another and build together in the spirit and in the natural.

As I mentioned before, Larry Joyner joined Salvation Christian Center sometime in 1992. He was a minister and close friend of the pastor (Melissa, my sister) and family; I knew of him through my family, since he was especially close them. Sometime during 1993, he invited me to his family cookout and also dinner with his family after a church service. On the way to dinner with his family, I told him that I had to drop by a bank to get money. He insisted that he pay for my dinner. My eyes stretched in amazement. I was thinking that this man could not be trying to hit on me since he had invited me to his family cookout, and now to dinner with his family. After the dinner invitation, I did not want to give him false hope so I stayed clear of him except for church related matters.

In August 1993, I had major surgery. Larry brought flowers to my home, which I thought was nice of him. I saw Larry as a relative, a nephew-type since he was close buddies with my nieces and nephews. It was challenging to get beyond the thought of him as more than an extended family member. Sometime in April 1994, he called to ask me to go out to dinner and a movie. When on the phone, I agreed after I told myself that he was not asking me to marry him, and then I remembered that I recently told a female friend that it would be nice to go out with a man for change, instead of just females.

Larry and I went to the movies and dinner and had a really good time. I felt good about it, until I got to church the next day and one of his cousins said that Larry told her that we went out. I acknowledged that we had, but I was livid because I am a private person about certain things in my life. I realize that being a preacher you do share some of your experiences, but not because you always want to. It was to be up to God and the Holy Spirit about how much we share and when. I talked to Larry about it later. I told him that if he wanted to see me again that my life had to be private between us. He agreed, although he did not fully understand. I did not want people to speculate that anything other than a platonic relationship was going on between us. We randomly dated because I was determined to reach my goals: to please the Lord by operating in ministry and getting my Ph.D.'s. I did not want any distractions in my life.

In November 1993, I began searching for a new home. This time I did not want to sell my condominium apartment and decided to keep it as a rental. I went to settlement for my new home in January 1994, but I did not move in until June 1994 to allow the sellers time for their new home to be built. I was so excited knowing that the Lord was blessing me abundantly. I know that my obedience allowed the Lord's blessings to flow. I really tried to be as obedient as I could because of my love for God.

Confirmation and Confusion

In the summer of 1994, Larry called me to ask if we could talk. I said okay. I said, "Jesus, don't let this man ask me to be his lady, as in girlfriend, because I am not ready for a commitment." I wanted to focus on my doctorate degree programs. When the day came to talk, I had to work late but he insisted that he still had to talk to me after I got home late from work. When we met, Larry started talking about things pertaining to us as a couple. I said to myself, "Jesus I know where he is going with this conversation." I reminded Larry that my policy is not to date men at the same church, not to date younger men, and that I did not feel comfortable since I knew his ex-wife and her family. He responded that his ex-wife and I were not friends, but just knew each other. I agreed, yet defended my stance with "but what about this and what about that." After all the "buts," there was nothing else for me to say. As he was preparing to leave, looking disappointed with my lack of responsiveness to him, he asked if we could go out sometime to the movies. I did not have the heart to disappoint him further, so I said yes. His impression was symbolic of the lighting of the White House Christmas tree—he lit right up. We did occasionally see each other and talked on the phone. I must say that he was patient and persistent with me.

Larry and I had fun together. There were times that he told me that he wanted to marry a woman with my characteristics. Again, I stretched my eyes because I knew where he was headed and I did not want to go there. I still did not see him as the type of man for me to marry. The dating continued sporadically, and we remained in a platonic friendship. In fact, Larry would stay at my home while I traveled for my job with the understanding that none of his things were to be left in my home when I got home. He became my best friend. We shared a lot of things with each other. It was refreshing to have a male best friend again in my life.

During my partying days in the 1970's, I had a male best friend, Ivan Jefferson. We were close, platonic friends. We talked at least two or three times per week. I was single and Ivan was married. For a season, we went to parties together. I met his first wife and likewise, he met every man that I had seriously dated. We always kept our friendship within proper boundaries, even when Ivan and his first wife divorced and later married someone else. Ivan and I had a disagreement between us that put a wedge in our friendship. Ivan wanted our friendship to be more than just friends, but I did not want our relationship to change, especially if our newly formed relationship did not work out. I missed my friendship with Ivan. But we both knew if we needed each other that the other would be there. I shared intimate things with Ivan as I would have with a female best friend, so I did not want to lose our friendship or him out of my life. We both were stubborn and the disagreement lasted for several years. What happened? After Ivan divorced his wife, he wanted us to have a girlfriend-boyfriend relationship. I said no, because I did not want to lose my best friend, besides I could deal with Ivan and his female friends as his best friends, but not while his girlfriend. Our broken relationship left a void in my life for several years.

Larry and I became best friends, and quickly filled that void. It felt good to know someone was there that I could really depend on and who cared about my well-being. Whenever I had to preach, he would take me to the location if he was available. Finally, the notion entered my mind about possibly marrying him since I would be marrying my best friend, a Christian man, preacher, and we could easily talk to each other about anything. We had fun together. I even disregarded the six-year age difference between us, the fact that we were members of the same small church, and that I was in a better financial and property assets status than he was.

In April 1996, Pastor Scott Madison, a revivalist from North Carolina was invited to Salvation Christian Center to do a revival. Pastor Madison, his wife, and adult daughter stayed at my house most of the time while he was preaching in the Washington, D.C. - Maryland area. After the last night of the revival, the pastor's daughter told me that her father wanted to talk to Larry and me at my house. I told Larry to come over and we met with the pastor that evening. He shared things with Larry and me about our relationship, which we had told no one. We knew only the Holy Spirit could reveal such detailed information. We listened, and then I cried because I was so head-strong and determined that I did not want Larry for more than just a good friend. Yet, the man of God said otherwise. I felt bad rejecting what the man of God said that God wanted me to have, as His blessing to me. I felt that he was not the one that God had prepared for me as a husband. We were both so overwhelmed by the conversation with the pastor and had to let everything sink in.

About a week after the Madison's visit to my home, I went to Williamsburg, Virginia and then to visit the pastor and his family in North Carolina. During my stay in the hotel room in Williamsburg, Virginia, I prayed for directions. I believe that God said that Larry was not the one to be my husband. He also told me to complete Continental Seminary that I had started in 1993. Now, I was confused because Pastor Madison said the Lord told him that Larry and I were soul mates. I rationalized my confusion by saying that Pastor Madison was far more spiritual than me so I should listen to him. I believed that God had told me that Larry was not the one, but I did not trust myself to stand on what I believed. Larry had already asked me to marry him two other times, and now a third time before I went to Williamsburg.

After I left Williamsburg, Larry met me on the highway to follow me to the Madison's house in North Carolina, which was en-route to his parent's house in South Carolina. I preached that Sunday morning at Pastor Madison's church. The anointing was very high and continued late into the evening with me ministering to people at the altar for several hours non-stop. After church we ate and I planned to return to Maryland and Larry, to South Carolina. I told Larry that I was drained, tired and sleepy. He suggested that I get a hotel room in North Carolina and travel back home the next day. I agreed and Larry stayed with me in the hotel room. We respected each other and nothing sexual happened between us. I said to myself that this man truly respects me and the anointing on my life. That night in the hotel room, we talked about what Pastor Madison had said to us, and I mentioned that a dear friend of mine liked him. Larry said that he knew, but he did not like her in that way. He stated that he wanted to be with me and not her. I told him that she was my close friend and I did not want our relationship to come between my relationship with her. We did not try to make any decisions at that time, but at least we had an honest conversation.

When I got back home, I began to act strange with Larry because I could not get out of my mind what I thought God had said to me in the hotel room in Williamsburg, and what Pastor Madison had said to us while in my house a couple weeks prior. Since I wrote what the Lord had shared with me in my journal, I showed it to Larry. Then Larry understood the change in my behavior and my reluctance about getting married. He did not agree that we were not supposed to be together and actually pursued me more to keep our engagement intact since he just proposed a couple of weeks prior.

Sisterly Conflict

Everyone we told about us getting married was so happy except my sister, Pastor Melissa. Her behavior became estranged toward me. It was like I was not her sister but a woman taking her son away from her, and I was not good enough for her son. Verbally she said she was for the marriage, but her behavior dictated a different message. I was happy, yet sad because I wanted everyone to be happy for us. I could not understand her behavior. I could not let it go. It bothered me severely, because I worked with my sister in her church and we never had a cross word between us and I was obedient to her as my leader. In church and around church folks, I always respected her as Pastor Snyder and not just as my sister Melissa.

I think the little girl within me wanted everybody to celebrate with me and I tried to understand why they did not. It was hard for me to let it go. After several months of confusion between my sister and me, Larry said to leave it alone because he knew that she would not change her position since her mind was made up about us, especially me. It did not matter how many times that I apologized to her, for whatever I was supposed to have done, it did not seem to work. I just wanted to bring harmony again between me and my sister especially since our mother told me years ago behind another family confrontation that she wanted her children to get along with each other. It did not work: it was eating at me as to why there was no resolution. My nerves were on edge.

At the time, I was still working on my Ph.D. programs at Hallelujah Christian Bible College and Continental Seminary, and working in an office with a manager that saw an area of low self-esteem in me and rode my back. I felt like her "whipping post." I made a decision that no matter how strained things were, I would focus primarily on my Ph.D. program at Hallelujah Christian Bible College and complete it. It was probably a way to distract myself from the deep emotional issues, as well as my commitment to finish since I had paid both colleges in full. Larry was afraid that I would give up on the relationship. At times, I said to him that it was not worth me losing my relationship with my sister or a close female friend for him. I had discussed my relationship with Larry, with my girlfriend. She was honest enough to remind me what I said on my mate desire list, that he must make an equal or better salary, be compatible in asset ownership. I agreed with her about what I had said, but I believed that he would get there and besides he said that he was not intimidated by my assets.

I tried to keep the conflict with my sister private since I was still going to her church. At times, the Lord reminded me that I was not supposed to return to Salvation Christian Center because that was not His perfect will for my life. I did not like being in limbo not understanding the will of God for my life. After a conversation between Melissa and I, she recommended that I return to the church until I understand the will of God for my life. In spite of the conversation between my sister and me, I felt the problem was due to my disobedience by returning to the church. But I did not know how to fix it. I even went to my sister's house with flowers to apologize again to try to resolve the problem, although I was still unclear what the problem was.

I just wanted the conflict and the distant relationship between us to go away. It seemed to work for a second, and then we were back at our distant relationship again. Sherita got Melissa and I together to try to resolve the problem, but I still could not understand why the problem would not go away. Melissa told Sherita if I had been disobedient to her that she would have sat me down and I would have sat down in obedience to her pastoral leadership. I remember one Sunday I was scheduled to preach, I got to church 10 minutes late for intercessory prayer and she did not let me preach. She had warned all of the ministers about being punctual for intercessory prayer on Sundays. I could not say anything or get upset—I was wrong. She preached. All of us ministers laughed because we knew she meant business. I discerned that my relationship with Melissa was bad, because she did not want me to marry Larry. Her behavior revealed that she was against us getting married, although her words stated she was in agreement with the marriage.

When Larry and I set a date in November 1996, we went to Pastor Snyder to tell her and have her bless our rings. She stated that we would get married when she said. This shocked us because she had not done that to anyone else that got married in the church, not even two of her children whose marriage ceremonies I performed for her so she could be a part of the ceremonies.

The next few months leading up to the wedding in November 1996 were more challenging. She did not want to talk to us together after the first session. Larry told me that she said negative things about me to him, and she told me that she hoped that Larry did not do to me what he did to his first wife. When I asked her what she meant, she said she could not tell me because it was confidential. I asked her why she brought the idea up in the first place. Later, one of my preacher friends, Evangelist Esther Malone, and another member of Melissa's church witnessed another conversation between us to resolve the confusion, but I could not understand why it continued. If my sister had given me just cause why Larry and I should not be married under better circumstances, I would have listened, but she did not. Her statements indicated that she agreed with the marriage, but her behavior stated that she did not agree with us getting married, but she refused to say why. We never got to the root problem of the confusion and I could not let go of my hurt.

My Marital Hopes

I married Larry because I loved him, and he was my best friend. I did not marry Larry because I was pregnant, because we did not have pre-marital sex. I had two homes, a good federal government job, two cars (most of the time), and traveled internationally and throughout the United States. I was working on two Ph.D. degree programs. I did not have to get married for the financial reasons. Larry had a car, lived in his family's home in Washington, D.C. with his sister and other family members. He was a police officer. After we got married he bought the family home from his father. I had dropped my mate desire list and did not make the comparison between my worldly goods and his worldly goods because I believed that we could acquire wealth together.

I was working primarily on one of my Ph.D. Programs, planning a wedding, working a full-time job and still accepting preaching engagements. I was tired mentally, physically, emotionally and spiritually. I found myself making all of the arrangements and finally one day I told Larry I could not do it anymore, and that he had to do more than just share the expenses of the wedding. He agreed and joined me in planning for and orchestrating the wedding.

In September 1996, Larry told me that he thought God wanted him to stay at Salvation Christian Center while I established the church that I felt God wanted me to establish in 1994. I told him that I did not believe that because if that was the case,

I did not need to get married to establish and pastor a church alone. Besides, I knew that Larry would be torn between me and my sister, his pastor—with whom we could not resolve our differences. If he stayed, I believed things would get worse instead of better. Larry would have been torn for his love for me and his loyalty for my sister. I could not deal with another problem and continue to work on my Ph.D. programs.

I was getting closer to the end of my Ph.D. program at Hallelujah Christian Bible College and I had to try to stay focused and cut back on the amount of distractions in my life. I told Larry that I thought that we needed to call off the wedding since my sister had plans for him in her ministry, which did not include me. He was upset, crying on the phone and said that he felt that God wanted us to get married. I told him to stay at Salvation Christian Center, but I could not handle the constant pressure any more. I was ready to throw in the towel and let him go completely. The roller coaster experience was too much for me. As a result, Larry and I agreed to get someone else to do the wedding. We both agreed that we did not want my sister to embarrass me on our wedding day by saying something negative during the ceremony. Before a Sunday morning service, we told her that we asked another pastor, David Jordon, to do the wedding and for her to do the communion portion and that the siblings were asked to wear our wedding ceremony colors of ivory and peach. She declined and said that she would not be there.

Neither Larry, nor I expected the conversation to turn out that way, especially since she was scheduled to preach. I told Pastor Snyder that she was my sister and pastor and that I would never do anything to hurt her or her church. I also said that if the break between us was not corrected, it would negatively affect the church and before I allowed that to happen, I would leave the church. She said, "Hmm," and walked out the back of the church to go into the sanctuary. That was my last Sunday at her church. She called me a couple of days later to ask why

I was leaving the church. I told her again that my decision was based on how our issues impacted the church, and I did not want to see the church in disarray because of our conflict. I hurt so badly because I could not understand my sister's behavior toward me. I wanted to let it go, but I couldn't. I took her emotions of rejection upon me. I kept apologizing, but it never worked even after Larry and I got married.

I was happy about getting married, but sad because of the strife between my sister and me that had torn our family apart. People were taking sides and telling me that she was jealous of me, and had said lots of negative things about me, and for me not to worry because the conflict was not my fault, but hers. Eventually, my family and friends did not want to talk or associate with me at all anymore. I was ostracized. I learned that others no longer wanted to be around the confusion, so they ceased to get involved. People fail to realize when you do not get involved and ceasing talking with either party that one of parties involved believes that you have sided with the other person by not saying anything. I was so hurt because I could not imagine what I had done except agree to marry the man that I loved, and who loved me. I spent a lot of time crying and confused because this should have been a happy time in my life, but it was instead a time of mixed emotions. I expected Larry to tell my sister, his pastor that he loved me, chose me to be his wife and I was first in his life. I felt like I was fighting over a man with my own sister, who was a mother figure to him. I still could not understand the confusion I was experiencing, nor how to fix the situation, even though I prayed fervently. Melissa and I will always be sisters, and we love each other, yet the confusion caused us to have a distant relationship.

The Rocky Start

A few days before our wedding, I got the flu. I was so sick. I thought about stopping the wedding, thinking, maybe this was a sign that we should not get married. In fact, the wedding dress that I found, which was supposed to be altered in the store, had not been done the week of our wedding. It eventually had to be delivered to my home. I was still nervous and wondering if I was doing the right thing. Yet I kept rebuking the devil, believing we would get the victory. The day before the wedding I called my sister Sherita at work to talk about my feelings. I told her how I felt and maybe I needed to cancel the wedding. She told me that it was too late to tell everyone. I thought about it and said she was right.

On November 2, 1996, I got married. I was a beautiful bride in my white dress, confident now that I was doing the right thing. Larry was a handsome groom in his white suit. The church was full of family and friends. My youngest brother, Gregory, walked me down the aisle until we got to the pew where my mother and father were seated, and then he turned me over to my father and mother to walk with me the rest of the way to the altar to give me away. I wrote our wedding vows, with Larry's agreement. Pastor Madison and his family came to the wedding and spoke words of encouragement and blessing during the ceremony. He shared with me before we left from my house for the wedding that if he had not come, then I would not have gotten married. He was right. I would have viewed it as him not standing by the word God told him concerning my marriage.

After the honeymoon, we talked so much about the confusion between all of us that I had to finally say "no more." I could not take it any longer and it was certainly not productive or pleasant to recall over and over again. I was still emotionally, spiritually and physically drained from everything that I was involved in my life. I feared that I would have a nervous breakdown or something awful would happen to me because of the stress on my body. Unfortunately, soon into our marriage, I had several bad dreams and tormenting spiritual experiences that I wondered if there was a wicked spirit in our bed with us.

Within the first year, I was already wondering if my husband was unfaithful to me. Over time, our intimate role as husband and wife decreased.

Other things happened that caused me to wonder about our marriage. In early 1997, my husband told me that he would get a loan to do some repairs to the Joyner family home in Washington, D.C. and to install a bathroom in our basement. Every time I asked my husband for the down payment to give to the contractor to start the work, he came up with excuses: "I did not get to the credit union today' or 'I was busy at work and could not get away." It was always something. I stopped asking after the third time because I did not want to hear any more excuses. I was disappointed because I felt that he had lied to me. I did not ask him to take out the loan. He told me that he did it because he knew that I wanted a second bathroom in the house. He was right about the bathroom, but right about little else—I could not understand the man that I married.

I thought we had healthy conservations about every area in our lives; after all, I had conducted several premarital and marital counseling sessions and taught a workshop on marriage at Hallelujah Christian Bible College. I told him that I did not mind changing the way that I had done business because I wanted us to be in agreement on how we do things in our home since it was no longer just me, myself and I—but we, us and ours. My husband and I discussed how much of the bills were for the home, his bills and my bills. I had to constantly remind him every two weeks for several months to give me money for the household expenses. I could not understand why he couldn't remember the money since he obviously remembered where he lived.

I soon faced the reality that I had disobeyed God and felt I was reaping the harvest of my disobedience. There began to be too many signs: the deception about the money, me reminding him to bring home his share of the money for household expenses, and my intuition or sense that there was the spirit of another woman in our bed. It felt like there was another presence in our bed while we were together. I prayed for that feeling to go away, but it wouldn't. My intuition kept leading me to believe that Larry was being unfaithful to me. I was still weak from the Ph.D. program—going non-stop with no significant breaks between classes, the confusion with Melissa, and working for a supervisor who I could not please no matter how much I talked with her and tried to do more for her. My mind went in all directions. I questioned myself repeatedly. I started not trusting myself concerning me, even though I believed I could trust hearing God regarding other people. Why am I married to a man that I am not sure of?

I often wondered who in the world was this man I was married to? I cried a lot from being lonely in my marriage. The caring man in our dating relationship became a different person within the first year of our marriage. The intimacy in our relationship had changed so severely and I asked him if he was having an affair. He said no, but even that did not agree with my spirit. I asked the Lord what else could happen. There were no answers, no relief and I was feeling more and more distorted. Eventually, I went to my gynecologist and then another specialist doctor that I was referred to determine if I had a female problem. Both doctors said no and asked me if anyone had molested me as a child. I shared all of the experiences that I stated in the beginning of my book. Then both asked if my husband was having an affair. When I told them that he said no, they both asked if I expected him to tell me the truth. I said yes I did because he is a Christian man and a minister. Both doctors smiled at me and said it was abnormal for us to be intimate so infrequently since we were still newlyweds. When I got home, I told Larry what the doctors said. Larry said that he disagreed with the doctors. But I continued to think that Larry had another woman in his life intimately besides me.

The Lump

Nevertheless, we started a church in March 1997. We both agreed to pastor although God had given me the vision for the ministry. I was still so tired mentally, physically, emotionally and spiritually that I did not fight the issue of him taking the lead with the church. But constantly I would hear God say that He had called me to pastor the church. Because I was tired, I told God that he needed to tell Larry because he thought the man should be the pastor. We started the church in the basement of our home with just the two of us. One Sunday, he would preach and I presided over the service and then the next time we exchanged duties and roles. Our first member was his niece, Linda Joyner. She came and started to work as our worship leader. As time went on, more and more people came. Some people from my sister's church talked about coming to our church and some came. I prayed and asked the Lord not to let them come unless He sent them. I did not want any more confusion because I was so tired.

In early September 1997, I discovered a lump in one of my breasts. I began speaking the word of God over my body and rebuking the devil for his work in my body. I asked Larry to pray, which he did the first time. After that, each time I asked him to pray for me, he told me that he already prayed about it once and that he did not need to pray about it again. I was shocked because I was his wife. I told him if I was one of the members at the church that he would pray with me as many times as I needed, so why not me. I was afraid for my life. Finally, I went to the doctor to see about it.

Larry was so emotionally detached about my health problem that I could not believe that this was the same man that I dated with so much compassion. The night before I had to go to one of my doctor's appointment, I called my youngest sister Jacquelyn and we prayed that the test results would be fine. Then I talked with Angela Jordan, a girlfriend of mine and we prayed for God's favor. Larry, lying beside me in bed, got out of the bed and slept downstairs. I had purposed in my heart that if I had to go through this ordeal by myself, that I would be by myself and there would be no marriage. His behavior was not a good indication of the compassionate man that I wanted to be with for the rest of my life. The next morning he came to the bedroom to tell me that the Lord told him that he needed to be more compassionate with me. I was still hurt because God should not have had to tell him something that should have been natural for a newlywed husband.

Larry went to a couple of my doctor's appointments with me. The week of the scheduled surgery, I talked with Pastor Doreatha Hawkins, my spiritual mother, of West Virginia and Bishop Daniel L. Knight from Nigeria. I was so encouraged by them that my attitude changed about the surgery and my well-being. Larry also decided to go to the hospital with me for the removal of the lump in my breast. I was very happy to have him with me, although I would have gone by myself if that had been the option. I told him that he did not need to stay, but he chose to stay and wait for me. The hospital staff that attended to me was amazed with my attitude because I had the biggest smile and positive attitude. I told them that I knew that Jesus was with me and that He would bring me through this ordeal.

My husband told me that I had "issues," so I began to think he was right and I sought counseling to help me to sort out my "issues." But it ended up that the problems were still there. I wanted to fix me so all of my marital problems would go away and I could have a happy marriage. I sought help because I did not want anyone to know that we were having marital problems. How could I be having marital problems? I counseled married couples (individually and together) and conducted pre-martial counseling sessions for many couples. How could I have missed it so badly? I arranged for us to go to marriage retreats, which he did not want to attend. I threatened that I would leave the marriage if he did not go. He went and later said that he was glad he had gone. The retreats provided several exercises involving self-reflections and exercises with each other. Following the retreats, the marriage was good for a while, and then reverted back to us living in the same house seldom communicating. We were limping along and holding on by a thin thread.

Marriage and Ministry

My drive to be an overachiever lost a lot of its punch in our marriage. I was emotionally drained because I could not understand what I had done to cause my husband to change his feelings about me. He had locked me out of his life, and I did not know how to get back in. He told me that I always had issues. It hurt because our marriage was my greatest issue. I wanted a good marriage. I wanted the type of marriage that he said that he wanted when we dated—a marriage admired by people. I cried many times behind the thought of that statement because I wondered where the man went that spoke it to me.

I was mad with everyone that said that Larry and I should get married. I had to quickly let it go because no one held a gun to my head or forced me to marry him. Just about everyone thought as I thought, that we made a nice couple and were destined to succeed in marriage. I accepted the blame for my mistakes in the marriage and found it hard to say positive things about it. It was quite a while before I could open up to people about my problems. Many of my closest friends and family had stopped talking to me after I felt they drained me of the details. One day the phone stopped ringing from concerned family and friends. I was all alone. No one was there except Jesus. I kept quoting the scriptures, "I have never seen the righteous forsaken, neither his seed begging for bread." I reminded the Lord that He would "never leave me nor forsake me,' and that 'I shall live and not die and declare His works." These passages of scriptures kept me alive because I constantly quoted them. With my own mental anguish, and not to mention that my mother kept telling me that she was afraid that I was going to have a nervous breakdown, it was only the Word of God that sustained me. At times, I battled to keep control of my mind from the constant and escalating hurt and pain that I was going through.

One day in 1997, I asked Larry if we should change the name of the church since God had given me the vision in 1993 and had it incorporated in September 1996 for the ministry as a means of hosting seminars for ministers, and later as a church (local assembly). Larry said no, to keep the name. I said okay. I wanted to be sure that he was okay with everything that we did. I wanted a peaceful marriage, as peaceful as it could be. A year after we started the church, we were installed as pastors by Bishop Sharon Miles, our spiritual covering. She asked who the pastor was. I told her both of us believed that God had called us during the course of our ministry to pastor. Bishop Miles listened and then said that only a monster has two heads. I told Bishop Miles that I did not want to offend my husband by not having him to pastor with me on an equal level. She installed both of us as pastors of the church. The membership grew and we eventually moved from the basement of our home to a building to continue the church assembly.

In the second year of our marriage, Larry seldom supported me when I had preaching engagements. I could not understand since he took me to my preaching engagements while we dated, even at times when his favorite football team was playing. I was baffled by the change. Was it because he finally got what he thought he wanted? I did not know. I just wanted my best friend back.

Into the third year of our marriage, Pastor Henry Gordon of Everlasting Life AME Church invited me as a guest speaker at a marriage retreat. We worked for the same federal government agency. We would say "praise the Lord" while passing one another in the hallway, and when he stopped by my office.

I was shocked and perplexed at the invitation because I was experiencing some serious issues in my marriage: finances, trust, responsibilities, and communication. I asked Larry to come with me, but he refused until I told him that Pastor Gordon wanted him to come. For the next two years, Pastor Gordon invited me as a guest speaker for his marriage retreats. Larry attended the second year also. I was honored to be a guest presenter, yet hurting inside, because I felt like a hypocrite since my marriage was not doing well. I remember praying and Jesus telling me that just because it seemed like His Word was not working in my marriage that did not mean that it didn't work. Those words were so profound because in troubles we often forgot the Word's power because we only see the problems. I understood that even in my test God would use me to minister healing to others. And He did. I was happy when the Lord used me to bring healing and deliverance in other's lives and marriages, yet I wondered about me and my marriage.

Larry and I had our ups and downs. But as a pastor I had to keep a victorious face for our church members and the public. During the course of my marriage, I was hurt by the betrayal, mistrust, lack of communication, abandonment, deception, lies and mistreatment by my husband. I was grieving during the course of my marriage because I could not believe that I had made such a mistake in getting married to him. I mainly blamed myself for the problems. I just wanted the problems fixed.

As much as I wanted to let the betrayal, infidelity, lies, deceptions, rejection, abandonment and lack of communication go; I could not because I could not understand why. Instead, the pain grew and I became a wounded woman with a deeply rooted hurting spirit. I did not want to hold onto the pain and the conflict from people whom I loved and cared about, but it grew into me operating in an unforgiving spirit towards former supervisors, Melissa and even Larry. I had to release all of the hurts and pain to be healed. They were challenging because I did not want a repeat performance by any of them. I was tired of being hurt and others acting as if I was entirely at fault. So I prayed a lot for the Lord to heal me completely.

Strangely, the Lord continued to use me mightily in church worship services, conferences and retreats to minister healing and deliverance to His people. Sometimes, Larry and I would team preach. I would preach first and then he would finish the sermon. He always wanted me to prepare our sermons. He stated that I could do it better than he could. I was a wounded soldier doing the work of the Lord. After the separation, and at various Christian services where I preached, people were shocked by my testimonies. They commented how they always saw me with a smile. I said, "Praise the Lord, then the Holy Spirit is doing His job because the joy of the Lord is my strength."

I Wanted Out of the Pain

Despite the smiles, I had to learn to release that unforgiving spirit so I could move on from my past. I had to find the root of my problem and stop seeing the person that caused the incident as the enemy. I learned to accept my part of the problem because I wanted the trial to be over and the relationship to resume as it was. I wanted the Lord to move my mountain as I certainly did not have the strength to climb the mountain. Unfortunately, the unforgiveness that I carried for a season gave birth to other negative ailments such as emotional problems (depression and anger) and physical problems (chest pains). I wanted peace in my life, but it was difficult to let go of the deep-rooted pain in my spirit.

I had to make a conscience decision to let it go. Anything that hindered my love for the Lord, I had to let go. I did not want anything to separate me from the love of God, nor did I want anything to hinder the flow of the anointing of God upon my life. I was being greatly used by the Lord, in spite of the behind the scenes problems that I was having in my life at home, church and work.

Before and even after we got married, Larry would not take me around certain people in his circle of friends, including those he worked with. He told me that he could not take me to his job because of the required security clearance, which I did not understand since my job required a security clearance. The only time that I met one of his co-workers was when she saw us a couple of times in the mall and she approached us. Thoughts ran through my mind. Was something wrong with me? Was I ugly to him? What was wrong with me? I tried to figure it out. Many times, I struggled in the marriage to make it work. At times, I wanted it to end because my husband told me that I had too many issues and placed the blame for the bad marriage primarily on me. I got professional counseling to find out how to fix me. Eventually, I got over the negative thoughts.

Many times, I thought I wanted out of the marriage because of his inept behavior and that he did not really want to be married to me. I felt terrible about my bad relationship, since I had waited so long to get married. I had experienced a lot and now I was prepared to spend the rest of my life with a husband, living a wonderful life in Jesus. I kept asking myself what I did wrong. I believed that if I knew what I did (the problem) then I could fix me with the help of the Lord by getting to the root of my problem. The pain hurt so bad that it penetrated my soul and spirit. I wanted it to stop immediately. I cried constantly for months. At times, I made myself sick by crying so much, and my stomach would be upset.

I talked with friends who were pastors and bishops to get counsel and insight about my marital, church and work relationships. I wanted my husband to love me from the heart as Jesus commands in the Bible. I wanted everyone to like me and to see the good in me. But the child inside still wanted to hold on to fear, insecurity, and wanted to be accepted. Several people told me to stop accepting the ill feelings of others toward me. However, I did not know how since I wanted everybody to like me. I thought by talking about it to my "friends" that it would ease the pain. It did for a brief moment, but it only returned the next time rejection occurred.

In 1999, I accepted a position in The Word Churches and Ministries Fellowship as an Overseer of Women's pastors. During our marriage, I continued to be the one who arranged for marriage counseling and marriage retreats in hopes to possibly saving our marriage. He would always initially reject going, but eventually give in to my request because he knew that I meant what I said about our marriage. I could not fix it by myself. I wanted him to want the marriage to work and put forth an effort to help it work. Eventually, in 2000, we went to Pastors Sam and Gloria Hampton of Holy Spirit Christian Center. We went for four sessions before he said that he would not go any longer. I poured out my heart at the sessions. I knew that I had better express myself clearly while I had his attention, because later I might not get the opportunity to be heard. While driving home from our last session, I confessed that I was jealous of the attention that he gave his family, portraying himself as a Mack-daddy, when it should be me that he tried to impress. He got mad and said that he would not go to any more counseling sessions and that I had the problem. Larry blew up at me and said that I did not trust him and it was a waste of time going to counseling. I told him that I was just being honest about my feelings. Afterwards, I realized that timing for sharing information was important. That was not the time for me to share my honest feelings with Larry.

In February 2001, I was asked by one of the senior bishops of The Word Churches and Ministries Fellowship to accept the position of bishop in the organization. I wanted to focus on Kingdom of God Ministries to get us to the next level in ministry as I felt the Lord wanted, so I did not share my vision with my husband. I worked diligently to move the church forward with his help, although it was challenging because I felt that he did not want me to know some things about the ministry. I knew that the new position would require a lot of my time. Since I split a lot of my time between church, serving as adjunct professor, and completing my dissertation at Freedom Christian University and Schools, I declined the position.

The Split

In March 2001, my husband decided that he needed a break from the church. He told me that he would not be there for the month of March. We had planned to celebrate the church's fourth anniversary the whole month. I asked him why? He said that he needed to get away to think about some things. He stated that he was going to get a hotel room in Williamsburg, Virginia. This behavior was abnormal for him. I asked him why not to get a hotel room in the area or go to the church while it was empty if he needed to think. He did not offer an answer. He came to the first evening service and did not come back until the last Sunday in March.

Every Sunday morning, I arrived at the church early for intercessory prayer. The first Sunday in March, the Lord asked me if everyone left the church, would I still preach. I told him I would since I knew that was not going to happen. He told me that He would raise up new people for me. Then He told me that He would have raised up new people for Moses, but Moses wanted to keep the people. So, every Sunday I made excuses as to why Larry was not at church. I did not lie, I just did not tell the whole story of why he was not there. I did not want to share information when I did not understand what Larry was doing or going through internally. I was so hurt because of his inept behavior about our marriage and us not working together as leaders of the church.

On the last Sunday morning in March, he asked me who was preaching, and I told him a guest preacher. He told me that he was coming back to church. I asked Larry not to have any part in conducting the service because it was not appropriate since we had been teaching the people to be responsible leaders in their position. I told him since he felt that he had to stay out for the month of March then he should sit down that morning. He came to church and sat in his position on the pulpit and respected my wishes. I acknowledged him, as this was the appropriate thing to do, but I did not allow time for him to talk. No one knew anything was going on between us until he told the members the next day. Later that night at home he gave me a letter of resignation from the church.

I wanted to write back quickly, but I asked God to help me to write because I did not want to say something that I could not take back. I gave Larry a reply on Friday of the same week stating that I accepted his resignation. I asked him how we could teach the members at the church to be faithful to the ministry, even if they are having troubles in their lives, when he stayed away from the church for a month so he could think and pray. I told him that I was his wife and sharing the pastorate, none of it made sense to me. I shared about the problems in our marriage and reflected back on the problems I saw in my parents' marriage, that I now saw happening in our marriage. I told him that I did not want our marriage to be detached because I wanted it to be all that God wanted it to be. I wanted my best friend back, but not the man who I was now married to.

Larry contacted the members during the week to tell them that he was leaving the church. The first Sunday in April 2001, I arrived at the church to see the church van parked in front of the church and the keys left on our desk. Larry and the church members, all but one, left the church. I remembered the Lord asked me if I would still preach, even if the people left the church. From April 2001 to January 2002, I preached every Sunday that I was in town whether anyone was there for me to preach to or not.

During this time, several pastors and bishops told me to give up the building and to continue the ministry with conferences and preaching platforms. I did not want to do that since the Lord was providing for all of the church expenses without me borrowing money from anyone. Pastor Jonathan Michael of Bible Baptist Church and Pastor Henry Gordon of Everlasting Life African Methodist Episcopal Church told me to call them if I got behind in the bills and not to take my household money to pay the church expenses. I told them that they need not worry about that because I did not want to get behind in my mortgage, especially since I was not getting any help from Larry, paying his part of the church lease. I continued to pay my tithes and household expenses. I was accustomed to two incomes and now I had to live again on one salary. I suffered lack, but I did not die in my winter because God supplied my needs.

After four years of co-pastoring the church, Larry decided that he did not want to be there with me anymore. He left and took 98 percent of the people: mainly his family, a few of my family members, and people who attended the church because of their association. The next week I shared the situation with Pastor Gordon. He told me to call a meeting to bring the people back to the church. I called the meeting as instructed. I wrote a letter to everyone to come to a church meeting, and I followed up with a phone call. I learned from Larry's sister, Priscilla, a former member of the church, that the members who left had a meeting with Larry and that everyone invited came. Of course, I was not invited, nor did I know about it until Priscilla told me on the phone a week later. She stated that the members decided to have their own fellowship and to remain separated from the church Larry and I had started. I sent Larry a letter inviting him to come also, but he refused and said that he would never come back to Kingdom of God Ministries.

Several former members came to the church meeting that I called, except Larry, Melvin, Darlene, Rebecca and a few other members. I discovered that Larry showed them a personal letter that I wrote to him for his eyes only. Not only had he betrayed me by secretively taking the members and holding a secret meeting, but he also shared personal and confidential information about my family and us. It hurt because I realized that I was sleeping with the enemy. Why was he so cruel to me?

I asked Pastor Gordon to facilitate the church meeting one Tuesday night in April 2001. Carroll Joyner (Larry's brother) and Marion Lancaster came ready to ridicule me. Every time they said something negative about me, one of their biological family members present said the opposite good things about me. At the end of the meeting, Pastor Gordon asked the people whom they saw as the pastor or visionary of the ministry. Everyone said Pastor Virginia. I could not understand the confusion except they were being loyal to their family member and friend, Pastor Larry. When I got home, Larry argued with me about Pastor Gordon facilitating the meeting. He stated that Pastor Gordon was an outsider facilitating the meeting and telling people to leave the church. I told him that Pastor Gordon had all of us form a circle for closing prayer, and then he said everyone who did not agree with Kingdom of God Ministries continuing to step outside of the prayer circle. I told Larry that Pastor Gordon did not tell anyone to get out of the church.

Carroll had called Larry before I got home to tell him about the meeting. I reminded Larry that Carroll and Marion were ready to attack me, but praise God for Pastor Gordon being there to help me. Several days went by before we talked. Larry eventually apologized for yelling at me about Pastor Gordon facilitating the meeting. He finally said that he was glad that Pastor Gordon did it for me. For several months, he would not tell me nor did I ask where they were meeting for church services. I could not believe this mess was in my home. The secrets, lies, betrayals, and little communication were too much for me. My heart hurt so badly. He kept telling me that the church members liked things the way they were—without me in the church. I said to him that he was putting the church people over me. I was depressed, yet I continued to preach God's Word every Sunday. I preached to the angels in the chairs and/or when someone decided to stop by for the worship service. I preached like I was preaching to thousands. I conducted a full service at times by myself.

A Congregation of One

Many of the members left when Larry no longer wanted to be with me at the church. I found myself alone at a church with one other person for the next nine months. The ill feelings in the home were too much to handle on top of the rejection of my husband and church family. What did I do? I felt like he had taken my baby from me and declared that I was an unfit mother without giving me a fair trial to defend myself. I finally realized that I could not control how my husband felt about me. I could only control how I felt about him and my attitude toward the situation. I prayed for God to help me because I hated my husband. I felt anger and hurt in my soul and spirit. The pain was too much. I felt like death was approaching me.

In May 2001, my sister Sherita told me to ask Larry to come back to the church, which I did. He said that he could not work with me. I asked him why. He said after I got my Ph.D. it was as if I went full speed ahead with the church. I told him he was right. I promised God that if He would help me through that dissertation that I would focus on the church, which I did. Even though I asked again, he said that he would never come back to Kingdom of God Ministries. He only came back to remove his personal things from the church before I returned the keys to the owner of the building.

I told Sherita where certain things were in case something happened to me. Then she stated that I sound like I was dying. This is when I realized that I was talking death. I never felt the urge to kill myself, but I had many thoughts of bad things happening to me to end my life or cause some awful affliction to me. I was very depressed because of the terrible circumstances in my life.

During this period, my Christian friends separated themselves from me. I felt that if I had committed adultery then I could understand, but I did not. Nevertheless, God gave me new Christian friends who accepted me. I could now count my old friends who stuck by me on one hand. I was still invited as a guest speaker to other churches' worship services, retreats, and conferences. After each invitation, I always told the senior pastor my status so that if he or she did not want me to come, then no problem. I did not want to portray a lie to anyone. I did not want to be a hypocrite. The anointing on my life had increased in spite of my hurts and pains. I was a wounded soldier preaching to help others to be healed.

I started as best I could on the process of learning to forgive my husband, family and friends for rejecting and abandoning me when I needed them the most. I felt that most people did not want my friendship or to be in my presence. I could not understand why when I did not cause the problem. I worked to make the marriage fruitful. Many times, I felt like going to a bar to get drunk or engaging in a sexual relationship with a man to bury my hurt and pain. But I remembered that Jesus said that He would never leave me nor forsake me, and He did not. So I could not temporarily leave Him when I needed Him the most. I kept putting one foot in front of the other to move on in life.

I had to deal with my anger from childhood to adulthood and release it so that I could start my healing process. I prayed to the Holy Spirit to show me myself. I realized that my anger did not start with my husband but God allowed the situation to bring the spirit of anger to the forefront so that I could deal with it to prevent it from being a hindrance in my life later. My life was a mess—at work, home and church. Where could I go? I cried out and asked the Lord to tell me what to do. I talked with Christian counselors to help me to sort out my life. I felt that a paid counselor would not have to think about my feelings as a friend, so I would be told what exactly the problem was. Maybe Larry was right after all and I was the problem. I did not want to hurt anyone. I just wanted to be loved unconditionally and to love likewise.

I realized that anger is something that everyone encounters. I realized that my anger occurred in various degrees from mild to extreme anger, causing varying degrees of harm to my spirit, body, and soul. The Bible says not to let the sun go down on your wrath. I initially experienced mild harm when I didn't cast my cares upon the Lord. The extreme harm came when I allowed the anger to cause bodily harm: a nervous stomach; difficulty in concentrating; trouble sleeping; uncontrollable crying at any time; wanting to lash out in anger at anyone who hurt me; and at times wishing those people would die or leave my life completely. The range of my emotions during this time of distress went from one extreme to the other. Nevertheless, I quoted Philippians 4:8: "whatsoever things are lovely and pure to think on these things..." and Romans 8:28: "For we know that all things work together for them that love the Lord, and are called according to His purpose."

Closed Building, Open Doors

In September 2001, I visited my friend Sylvia Bates in Oakland, California. I was scheduled to be there for a week with a return flight on September 11, 2001. I enjoyed my visit with Sylvia in spite of my heart still hurting so badly on the trip. I continued to deal with mixed emotions of wanting, and not wanting our marriage to work, since I waited until I was over age forty to get married. I stilled loved Larry in spite of what happened between us. I kept asking myself over and over in my mind, why did this happen? How did I get to where I am? What could I have done to prevent it, especially when I should have known better, since I had counseled single and married couples about relationships? I could not believe that I made such an awful mistake by marrying Larry. I was upset with Pastor Madison, and anyone else who told me that the Lord wanted us to get married. Then one day, I stopped blaming everyone else and put the blame where it belongs—with me. I said yes to Larry to get married and no to God not to marry Larry. I had to learn how to forgive God and myself.

I was caught in the September 11 ordeal and could not return home for several days. I called home to see if Larry had called me—he did not. However, one of his co-workers, who did not know we were separated, had called to see if I was alright because she thought I worked at the Pentagon. That hurt. I felt like I meant absolutely nothing to the man that I had been married to for almost five years. What did I do that turned him against me? A couple of weeks later he came to get his mail. He talked about how he was in South Carolina visiting his parents when he heard the news about the Pentagon in Washington, D.C. and the Twin Towers in New York. He said that he called home to make sure that his cousin who worked at the Pentagon was all right. Then he asked me about being caught up in the traffic during that time. I said I did not have that problem as I was in Oakland, California praying to get home safely. Larry just said "oh," moved on to another conversation, and then left my house.

While at a retreat in October 2001, a prophet, who did not know me nor my situation, prophesied to me to keep the doors open, and that the people would return. I tried to walk by faith, but I gave up hope. At the end of December 2001, I contacted the owner of the building we rented for our church to tell him what happened. He was disappointed and wanted me to stay. I told him that I made him a promise when I signed the lease to pay him for the next three years, which I did. He told me that he appreciated my commitment to our agreement. I closed the church building on January 31, 2002. God did not tell me to close the church, but I asked God to allow me to come aside to be healed. I believed that my spiritual and emotional state would prohibit me from being an effective pastor. I did not want to hurt other people unintentionally while I was trying to heal from my wounds. I did not realize that God wants to sometimes heal us where we are.

One type of ministry door closed, but other ministry doors and opportunities were opened to me. I was so happy because I could focus on helping other people, which in turn helped me not to focus on my problem. If God had stopped me from preaching then I would have thought that He hated me like Larry. I think that I would have had that nervous breakdown that my mother was concerned would happen to me.

In January 2002, I talked with Pastor Mark Fisher of Power of Faith Christian Center, our spiritual mentor, about the situation. Larry mainly talked with Pastor Fisher about church business since they periodically went to lunch while I was at work. Larry presented any questions that I had for Pastor Fisher and shared with him what we were doing in the ministry, and then share their conversation with me when he got home.

Pastor Fisher was surprised, although he had heard somewhat, of the situation. I told him that I wanted to come to his church to be healed because I was so wounded from the many non-stop circumstances that I had encountered over the years. He agreed and shared his expectations of me as a minister in his church. After the church assembly discontinued, I went to Power of Faith Christian Center for about a couple of years to blend in the crowd as a parishioner, still hurting and trying to discern the will of God for my life. I sat and listened to the Word being preached from Pastors Mark and Diamond Fisher and their assistant and associate pastors. I needed spiritual nourishment.

The Lord used two prophets to give me the same prophesy in 2002. One prophet was a guest speaker at a women's conference in Pennsylvania and the other a friend who lives in North Carolina. Both prophets told me that the Lord said that I had not lost anything. I could not understand because my marriage had failed, the church folks had left the church and I was hurting— what did He mean? Later, I realized that if Larry had been the man for me, then we would be together. In spite of the negative circumstances in our marriage, we would have allowed the Lord to help us to work them out.

The Divorce

Soon after our separation, I started hearing things about Larry. I heard that he got a woman pregnant while we were in our first year of marriage. Unfortunately, it was someone that I know. The child was about six years old when I heard it. I was so hurt and shocked. All I could think is that he gave to another woman what I wanted in our marriage. Discovering his secret helped me understand the money problems that Larry had paying bills at home and keeping his commitments to me. Some of the old members began to tell me things about the church split. I told them that Larry told me they did not want me to be at the church with them—everyone denied that as the truth. I shook my head and asked God why?

After we had been separated for a year, I contacted Larry about a divorce. Up to that point, the only time we talked about anything was when he had mail that came to my address. I did not want to continue to live in limbo, a limbo that lasted from 2001 until the divorce became final in 2004. I hurt so badly and I was lonely. This was not an unusual feeling because I felt lonely while Larry and I lived together as husband and wife. I wanted the Lord to stop the pain – to make it go away. However, God did not take away the pain, but helped me to grow through the pain to the point I could talk about it in an open forum to help others. God helped me to release the past so that I could move on to a better life and to stop any regrets of my past. I had many regrets. At times, I found myself pondering repeatedly why and what happened. The only answer that I had was that Larry was sure about what he wanted and it wasn't me, and that I could not make him love me.

I continued to work on myself by attending retreats, reading my Bible and inspirational books, fasting, worshiping and praising the Lord through prayer and sharing with others because I did not want to take the baggage of negative memories into another relationship. This would not be fair to someone else, nor me in a new relationship. I did not want flashbacks once I saw any behavior that reminded me of Larry in another relationship. I had to learn to let it go and get rid of all soul ties to Larry.

I finally called Larry to tell him that I was filing for a divorce. I thought it was the right thing to do since we only talked when he picked up mail. He said that he wanted to talk with me. I told him he could come over later, and that I would call him when I got home. I had an appointment with an attorney to start the divorce proceedings. I told him that I was a Christian and a pastor and I felt badly about filing for a divorce. The attorney heard me and told me not to worry. I told the attorney that Larry and I signed a three-year rental contract on the church building. He said that if Larry came after me for anything that we could have him pay back all of the money that he should have helped pay since he breached the contract. The attorney saw that I was undecided, yet hurting. He told me that I needed to move on with my life without him. I could understand what he was saying, but that did not take away the mixed feelings that I had as a Christian.

When I got home, I called him. He came over to talk about reconciling the marriage. I was surprised since his behavior gave me the impression that he did not want the marriage any more. He said that he was sorry for how he treated me. He said that his life was not right and that he wanted to be in God's will. He said that he wanted his family back. I asked him what he meant by family. He said us. He said that he knew he did not talk to me much and he stayed in the basement while I was upstairs. He said that he would talk to me more since he knew that I liked to talk to him. He said that Sunday that I came to his church he knew that I came to see if he had another woman.

I said I did because I could not believe that a marriage would break up over a church.

He further told me that he went along with what the people who left the church with him wanted. He said that they did not want things to change. I asked how he could put the people before me—a big problem in our marriage. He said that he talked with the people after the Sunday that I came to his church and told them he wanted to get back with me. He said they told him if I came back they would leave. I said, "What? Then they will not have to worry that I am coming to your church because I won't unless God tells me to do so." He said that he told the people that they could not tell him what to do about his marriage because it was separate from the church. I told him that he made them a part of the decision-making process when he allowed them to come between us to start another church, and to allow them to say whatever they wanted to say about me. A couple of the members that left the church told me some of the conversations that people had about me. He said that they did not have anything to do with us getting back together.

I listened to him. It was challenging not to say something. I had so many questions to ask, but he told me during the time we were together that I would not let things go. I told him that I just wanted answers and the truth. He left my house with the decision left up to me about the continuation of our marriage. I told him that I would pray. He agreed to give me time to decide. I agonized as to whether I should or should not stay in the marriage. Could I fully forgive him for the betrayal, abandonment, lying, cheating, and mistrust? I thought about it a lot. I thought about a couple of my friends that took their husbands back after adultery. I thought about the powerful testimony it would be of all that I went through and how God healed both of us individually and our marriage. I was afraid, but I could see us getting back together since God used me as a guest speaker in several marriage retreats. I felt that if I could minister hope and healing to others, I could surely have the same blessing. I took several days to think about it and finally gave him an answer: yes—even though I was nervous about it because I did not want to get hurt again.

During the period February 2002 to November 2002, Pastor Fisher talked with us a few times about our marriage, separately, once on the phone while Larry was in his office, and finally at his home. In November 2002 at the final meeting in his home, he asked Larry what he wanted to do. Larry said that he was ready to move on. Then pastor asked me and I said that I wanted a husband who wanted me. He was disappointed in our decision to let the marriage go. I greatly appreciated the efforts of this man of God during the time of our separation because he was one of five clergy who tried to get my husband and me together to talk about the problems in our marriage. The other four were Pastors Sam and Gloria Hampton, Pastor Henry Gordon and his wife and Pastor Clinton Woods of Living the Word Christian Center. It seems as though others were afraid to touch the subject. I could not understand why. Maybe they felt that it was not their business. The moment they listened to me telling them my problem, I made it their business to lend some sort of support. They should have told me that they did not want to hear my business—I would have respected their wishes and not told them about my personal troubles. I reached out to people hoping and praying for a hand of fellowship. It is unfortunate how unwilling even Christians can be in reaching out to another in time of need.

Reconciliation?

One Sunday morning in August 2002, Larry and I agreed to meet after the 8:00 a.m. service at the Power of Faith Christian Center. During that service, Pastor Fisher asked Larry to come to the front of the church. He proceeded to tell the church that he wanted Larry to come in as a sitting pastor until he received direction from the Lord on what to do. During his talk, he called me to the front of the church. He proceeded to tell the church that we had a church together as husband and wife. He said that he did not ask us if he could say what he was getting ready to say, because if he did we would probably say no. So he told the congregation that he had talked with both of us separately. He stated that he felt the Holy Spirit was leading him in a different direction. He had an altar call for all the married couples in the church that were thinking about divorcing, separating, or having problems. Several couples came forward. Pastors Fisher prayed for each couple that God would heal their marriage.

After church, Larry and I went to breakfast to talk about our relationship. We discussed what had just happened at the church. Larry said that he was not sure if he wanted to get back together. He said that he was going to Myrtle Beach, South Carolina for a week and that he would think about it. I thought that it was strange for Larry to go to Myrtle Beach by himself. This was out of character for him, but I did not address it. In fact, I told him that I had a coupon for a three-day stay in Myrtle Beach if he wanted it. He said that he was staying a week. Later that evening, Larry and I talked on the phone. He said that Sonya, his sister talked to him about the service and that he told her that he was not sure what he wanted to do about reconciling the marriage. I told him that I felt like a yo-yo—that he was jerking me around because he did not know what he wanted in the marriage.

In September 2002, Larry and I went out again a couple of times to talk about our relationship. He told me if he came back that he knew that he would have to help me with the bills. He said that he had to pay the mortgage at his house in Washington, D.C. I asked him why since his sisters were staying in the house with him. I said the rent they were paying him should help to cover most of the expenses. Larry said nothing. Then I said yes, I expect you to help with the expenses when you come back. Although we talked about reconciling our relationship, he never moved back home.

In October 2002, we committed to reconciling the marriage and I stopped the divorce proceedings. One night, Larry came over to visit. We talked and then our passion for one another took over. Before we made love, I asked Larry if he was serious about us reconciling our marriage, he said he was. I knew if we had made love, then Maryland law requires that we would have to wait another year before proceeding again with the divorce. Then I asked him to please not consummate the separation period in the marriage, because if he was not serious, having sex would by law, mandate that we wait another year before filing for divorce. He said that he was serious and spent the night. The next morning while lying in his arms, I asked him what happened in our marriage. I told him about my jealousy of his family since it appeared he was more concerned about caring for them than me. I asked him if it was because he was jealous of me. He said that he did not want to talk. I got upset. I was upset and disappointed. I told him if we did not talk about the issues that it was inevitable that the problem would happen again since we were only dealing with the symptoms. He said that he did not want to talk about it. I got quiet. I kept thinking that I did not want to go through that all of that hell again later because we did not deal with the root of the problem now.

One night in November 2002, Larry and I had an appointment to talk with Pastor Fisher as a follow-up in our marriage. I called Pastor Fisher and told him what I had done when Larry came to my house and that Larry and I decided to move on. He said that he wanted to talk to both of us at his house. Larry and I had not talked much since our last night together. I could not let it go that he did not want to talk about the problems that caused us to separate. That night at Pastor Fisher's house, he asked us what happened and that he was sorry that he left us alone, but he thought that we were doing fine. I told him we were not living together, which he was surprised. Larry told Pastor

Fisher that he was ready to move on. Pastor Fisher told Larry that whatever unresolved problems he had in this marriage, he would take them into his next marriage.

He told Larry that he should try to work things out. Larry was adamant that he did not want the marriage. Pastor Fisher asked me if I wanted the marriage and I replied that I wanted a husband who wanted me. When we prepared to leave Pastor Fisher's home, he told Larry to walk me to my car since it was dark outside. When we left Pastor Fisher's house, I called Larry on his cell phone to ask him if he wanted to go some place to get something to eat. He said no. We did not contact each other again from November 2002 to April 2003.

In April 2003, Larry's father died. My mother-in-law had Phyllis, another one of Larry's sisters call me. I had a major operation a couple of weeks prior and I could not drive since the travel to South Carolina would be too much strain on my body. I called Larry to give him my condolences. He thanked me. I told him that I would like to go to the funeral because I cared a lot for his father, but because of my surgery I was unable to attend. He said that he knew, because my sister Melissa had told him. He said that she asked him if he was going to call me and he told her no. I asked him why. He said that he did not want to give me the wrong impression by calling to see how I was doing. I told him that I would have thought that it was nice of him to call me to inquire how I was doing. I felt bad because it showed me just how much this man did not want me nor if he really loved me. I wondered if he ever did. How could a person flip so much to the opposite extreme? I remember when I was all that he wanted.

During our conversation, he told me that he was moving to South Carolina and not coming back to this area because he wanted to start a new life. I was hurt by his behavior even though we were not living together as husband and wife. I was so glad that God had ministered to me a few days prior that He would supply all of my needs. I held onto that promise whenever I felt lack in any area of my life, including loneliness. I learned that God is truly Jehovah-Jireh, my provider.

In April 2003, I filed for the divorce again with a different Law Firm. This time it was too early to file. The lawyer told me that I had to wait until October 2003 for the paperwork to enter the court to start the procedure. I told her that I just wanted to put the paperwork in to get it over with and move on with my life. Larry had left the Washington, D.C. area to relocate to South Carolina. He told me that he did not plan to return to Washington, D.C. I heard that loud and clear. I knew in my heart that it was over, yet I had a little gleam of hope that things would work out for us if it was God's will. I did not want to go through a divorce and everything associated with it. I wanted the pain to go away. I wanted my peaceful life back.

It's Over

When it was time to serve the divorce papers, I had to locate Larry in South Carolina. When we talked, he graciously provided me the information I needed. In fact, it was frightening because he talked to me as he did while we were dating. I was glad that he was accommodating to me during this matter. We apologized to each other for our parts in the marriage break. He told me that God had dealt with him about me while he was in South Carolina. He told me that the breakup in our marriage was not my fault. I asked him what happened as I did not want to repeat it again in my next marriage. He said the problem was his pride. He asked if I planned to get married again. I said yes, that he had not traumatized me to the point that I did not think that I could do it again. Besides, I knew that I could make some man a wonderful wife. He told me that he did not know if he would get married again. I listened to him talk, knowing that I was told that he started dating another woman immediately after relocating to South Carolina. Why the lies and betrayals?

In October 2003, I found out that Marion Lancaster, one of the former members of our church had cancer. She was one of the members who came to the church business meeting ready to ridicule me instead of discussing the future of the church. She saw Melvin, my nephew and Larry's best friend and his wife at a store. She asked them to have me call her. When I called, she told me that she had cancer and that she wanted me to pray for her, which I did. I felt that this was her way of apologizing for her part in the church split, although she did not say it. The Lord blessed me to forgive her instantly. She told me she had not told anyone outside of her family about the cancer. I continued to call and check on her even while I was out of town. In February 2004, she told me that the other church members had called. She stated that she had not heard from them since Larry discontinued his church around July 2002.

In the course of our conversation, she told me that Larry's family told her that he was involved with another woman, and who she was—the same information I heard the year prior. When I heard it again from a different source, and knew that the two individuals did not talk to each other, I knew that the information must be true. Then she told me that Larry broke up the church over the woman. I laughed and agreed that he broke up the church over a piece of booty. She asked me to forgive her, which I did. I told her that I felt she had non-verbally asked for forgiveness when she called and told me about the cancer. She said that she told the other former members that the next time that we talked that she would ask me for forgiveness. She said that they were surprised that we had been talking and I had been praying for her.

On another occasion Marion asked me to go to New York to do her funeral when the time came. She explained that it was the wish of her and her husband. I agreed and kept asking God what I could possibly say. I still had some residual hurt in me that God had to deal with and He did. In April 2004, I went to New York to officiate Marion's funeral. In fact, I did the whole ceremony except to sing. I praise God for the test of forgiveness. Larry called me one night to tell me that Marion had passed. I told him I knew and that I went to New York to officiate the funeral. He was surprised. I had to learn to let it go so that I could move on.

CHAPTER 5

A SETBACK FOR A COMEBACK

It is a Part of God's Plan

Virginia Harrison

I am where I am for a purpose.
I am here for a reason, season or to stay.
GOD has a purpose for my life.
I survived my trials because HE has a
plan for me to succeed.
All setbacks which include a bad marriage,
bad relationships with friends, family,
church members, co-workers, and supervisors;
the death of loved ones and close friends, the
negative thoughts, disappointments or the
lack of support when I needed it the most;
It is part of God's plan.
I choose to release and let go of all past hurts,
*   misunderstandings*
and grudges because they are distractions to keep me from
focusing on my purpose, to keep me from taking good
care of my body—the temple of God
and to keep me from God's best for my life.

To let it go is a part of God's plan for me to succeed.
I am here for a reason, season or to stay.
I am blessed because I know that God has a
plan for me to succeed.
My setback is a setup for a comeback.
I made it back because I am blessed!
God has a plan for me to succeed
according to Jeremiah 29:11.

My whole life had shifted. I felt I was in the wilderness trying to find my way out to the Promised Land. God wanted to take me to another level or dimension in His presence and intimate relationship with Him. Yet, I could not understand initially because I, the woman, who was a minister and pastor was divorced. I could not look to the left or the right; I could only look up to Jesus for my help. No matter how many times I got advice from others, especially clergy friends, I found myself relying on Jesus to bring me through the pain, shame, embarrassment, guilt, rejection, abandonment and feeling unworthy, to preach the Word of God.

God permitted me to experience the wilderness to bring me into a Canaan land, flowing with milk and honey. But I could not see it. All I could see was separation and abandonment from people that I loved and cared for. I was lonely, but I learned to turn to Jesus for companionship. During that time, I learned how to enjoy being with me; and I learned to fall in love with myself and to stop allowing people to treat me with disrespect.

God had to allow me to go through the wilderness in order to use me to continue the work for His kingdom. I could not see how, but I had to believe that everything that I experienced in the wilderness would work for my good.

"And we know that all things work together for good to them that love God, to them who are the called according to his purpose." (Romans 8:28, KJV)

I experienced spiritual warfare, extended times of waiting, pain, rejection, and isolation. I had to go through that process if I wanted to be used mightily by the Lord. The anointing is costly and demands the sacrifice of your life for Jesus' life. It involved laying down my life for Jesus, and taking up my cross and following Him.

I went from notoriety in ministry to humiliation in ministry and my personal life; from a very comfortable means of economic resources to very limited resources to possibly returning my car back to the dealership to avoid repossession; from a marriage to no marriage; from activity and action to inactivity; from socializing to solitude and loneliness; and, most importantly—waiting ... and waiting ... and more waiting.

I cried, complained and wondered when God would bring me out of the wilderness. The Holy Spirit told me not to complain but to praise God in the midst of my trials. It was difficult, but finally, one day at a time, I experienced praising Jesus above my pain. Even so, I still had challenges leaving my past to move forward with the purpose that I have been placed here on earth.

God is still preparing me today for His purpose. Everyone's circumstance is different; yet the end result is to go through the trials and walk in victory. The time frame for my wilderness may not have been quite as long if I had yielded early in the process. But the characteristics of the training are still the same. I had to learn not to prolong the wilderness time through disobedience or to shortcut the experience due to impatience—only leading me to cul-de-sac experiences, which forced me to revisit the lessons I was meant to learn earlier. I learned to embrace my trials, so that God could use my life for something extraordinary.

I had to learn to stop holding myself in bondage to what other people thought about me. I had to learn how to affirm myself. I wrote affirmation statements in a notebook for myself to read daily. I said to myself that I am special, wonderful, and unique. I had to realize that people do not just arbitrarily dislike you. It may be something they see that you have that they want, or they desire to be like you. Everyone, at some point, desires something that someone else has. We are human beings. Adam and Eve started it in the Garden of Eden when they desired to take of the fruit from the tree that God told them not to eat. This is what makes each of us strive to be better, when we see someone we admire, doing better. It encourages us that we can do likewise. Sometimes, we can ask the person for help and other times, we can read their published work to see what they did and do likewise. We all have something that someone wants or even needs; otherwise we would not be unique and wonderful. Only a fool will try to take from a person who has less than he or she has. Nine out of ten thieves will steal from a person who has more than they have.

Life is full of opportunities, promises, and challenges. We are encouraged to go after them. We must not allow distractions to stop us from reaching our goals, dreams, aspirations, and visions. I had to struggle through the intensity of pain and not allow my dreams, visions and goals to die because people disapproved of me. I had to realize that they were only distractions from the devil allowed by God. I struggled with letting go of the past to embrace my future. I kept analyzing things because I wanted to know the root cause so that I would not have a repeat performance of circumstances in my life. I had to let go of my hurt and pain, and affirm that God would get all the glory for the great things He has done in my life. I have a purpose in life. I am somebody in Christ. He loves me, so I had to learn to love myself enough to stop other people from mistreating me.

1. Embrace challenges as opportunities

I needed to view my setbacks as part of the process that I must accept rather than circumstances that I reject and ask God to remove. I had to see them as opportunities for God's miraculous plan to bless me. I had to embrace my challenges as opportunities. I realize that some of my adversities were more challenging than others; nevertheless, I still need to look at my circumstances and realize that Jesus is doing something great inside of me—transforming me into His image and likeness more and more every day. My flesh dies daily to embrace a great spiritual relationship with Jesus. If I did not have setbacks, I could not appreciate how Jesus could orchestrate my life with a great comeback as I put my trust in Him to bring me through.

2. View failure from a different perspective

I learned from my failures as well as from my successes. Not every failure in my life meant a defeat nor did it mean that I was a failure. Rather, it meant that I needed to look at the situation from a different perspective. I had to set my affections on things above and not on things on the earth:

"If ye then be risen with Christ, seek those things which are above, where Christ sitteth on the right hand of God. Set your affection on things above, not on things on the earth. For ye are dead, and your life is hid with Christ in God. When Christ, who is our life, shall appear, then shall ye also appear with him in glory" (Colossians 3:1-4, KJV)

3. Embrace a positive mindset

I had to praise God to overcome depression. I had to change my thinking, perspective, attitude and actions if I wanted to continue to succeed in life.

"If thou faint in the day of adversity, thou strength is small" (Proverbs 24:10, KJV).

4. Be strong during the battle

I did not want to faint in the time of my adversity. Nevertheless, I struggled until I could learn to set my affections on things above. I had to be persistent to fight the good fight of faith.

"And let us not be weary in well doing: for in due season we shall reap, if we faint not" (Galatians 6:9, KJV).

5. Be confident about your gifts and talents

I kept saying, "I can do it." I kept telling myself that God had put purpose inside of me. He had given me many talents and gifts, and surely He did not allow me to get all of this education and life experience just for nothing.

"Being confident of this very thing, that he which hath begun a good work in you will perform it until the day of Jesus Christ" (Philippians 1:6, KJV).

6. Press forward to accomplish God's (Jehovah Gmolah) plan for your life

I had to change my mindset to bounce back from my setback. This means that He has equipped me to accomplish great things. I finally realized who I am and whose I am. I had to press forward to accomplish God's plan for my life. I had to see myself as Jesus sees me—an anointed and accomplished woman of God who is destined for greatness.

"Finally, brethren, whatsoever things are true, whatsoever things are honest, whatsoever things are just, whatsoever things are pure, whatsoever things are lovely, whatsoever things are of a good report; if there be any virtue, and if there be any praise, think on these things. Those things, which ye have both learned, and received, and heard, and seen in me, do: and the God of peace shall be with you." (Philippians 4:8-9, KJV)

7. Acknowledge your weakness to God (Jehovah El Shaddai)

My response to adversity said much about my character. I found out more about my character by my emotional reaction to events. Was I as close to Jesus as I thought? No. Was I standing on the Word of God and not allowing fear to separate me from the love for Jesus? Not always. A sign of maturity is recognizing weakness, confessing them to Jesus, and acknowledging that you need Him to continue to improve your relationship with the Lord.

8. Walking in obedience to God (Jehovah Nissi) brings victory in your life

What the devil meant for harm, God turned it around for my good, because I am His child and especially when I operate in His obedience. This is how God takes care of me. I love being spoiled by Jesus. This is why I want to obey Him. When people set out to hurt or harm me, I pray for them that God will bless them. Truthfully, it was challenging and humiliating to do, but I had to forgive in order to walk in victory. In doing so, God will avenge them on my behalf. God wants my attitude to be right with him.

9. God (Jehovah Jireh) will protect His children

God looks out for me even when I mess up and turns my setbacks around to bless me and work for my good. God will do the same for all of us. I had to learn to trust Him blindly to bring me through my adversities. My setbacks were a setup by Jesus for a comeback. My life is in His hands. He will use my adversities and triumphs to bless others.

"For I know the thoughts that I think toward you, saith the LORD, thoughts of peace, and not of evil, to give you an expected end. Then shall ye call upon me, and ye shall go and pray unto me, and I will hearken unto you. And ye shall seek me, and find me, when ye shall search for me with all your heart. And I will be found of you, saith the LORD: and I will turn away your captivity, and I will gather you from all nations, and from all the places whither I have driven you, saith the LORD; and I will bring you again into the place whence I caused you to be carried away captive." (Jeremiah 29:11-14, KJV)

10. Maintain a champion mentality

If I have faith in Jesus Christ to work everything out for my good then a setback is only a set up for a comeback. I had to learn and then maintain a champion mentality. I had to have a positive outlook in the face of oppositions and adversities.

"No weapon that is formed against thee shall prosper; and every tongue that shall rise against thee in judgment thou shalt condemn. This is the heritage of the servants of the LORD, and their righteousness is of me, saith the LORD" (Isaiah 54:17, KJV).

11. Stand in faith on the Word of God

God promised us that weapons—those evil darts that Satan will form against us to hurt us, will not prosper if we stand on the Word of God. This is why we must do as Jesus did against Satan and use the Word of God as our weapon of defense. Satan's kingdom is not afraid of us when we speak the Word of God. His kingdom is afraid when we stand on the Word of God in faith.

Our faith in God's Word pulls on His compassion and mercy and He brings glory to our lives. Things come to try us—not to kill us.

"There hath no temptation taken you but such as is common to man: but God is faithful, who will not suffer you to be tempted above that ye are able; but will with the temptation also make a way to escape, that ye may be able to bear it" (I Corinthians 10:13, KJV).

12. Demonstrate resilience in Jesus

Jesus will use these trials and adversities to build His character in me so that I can carry out His Great Commission. I had to learn not to allow the little girl to control the woman in me but allow the child to be healed and mature, to not be afraid when the devil comes to try me.

114

13. Turn your scars into stars

I learned how to turn life's trials and adversities into victory to be an overcomer and more than a conqueror. I learned to turn my scars into stars and rise to the occasion of my purpose in the situation. I learned when given a lemon, than I must turn it into lemonade—to look for opportunities to show forth the miracles of God in the situation. I learned how to look at a situation and decide I would have the victory and not be defeated. I had to choose my battles, but not fight them all. Satan will weary us to give up if we try to fight them all. I learned to do spiritual battle in prayer, the place where the battles are won.

"Finally, my brethren, be strong in the Lord, and in the power of his might. Put on the whole armor of God, that ye may be able to stand against the wiles of the devil. For we wrestle not against flesh and blood, but against principalities, against powers, against the rulers of the darkness of this world, against spiritual wickedness in high places." (Ephesians 6:10-12, KJV)

14. Maintain a victor mentality and not a victim mentality

I am a victor in Jesus and not a victim. I got this in my spirit, and I repeated it as often as I needed to avoid a depressive spirit from influencing my behavior. Adversities are not setbacks, but opportunities for God's power to be manifested in our lives. We must use God's formula for success, the word of faith to consistently turn those setbacks into comebacks. In every situation, we must seek to see the opportunity for victory. We need to turn our obstacles into opportunities. In all of life's situations, we must look for the power of defining moments that will change our lives and show us how we can make the most of those moments.

CHAPTER 6

LET IT GO!
(Affirmations)

I AM FAIREST AMONG WOMEN

Virginia Harrison, Ph.D.

Jesus searches for His bride until He finds her. He does not discriminate because we are different from one another in status, complexion, or appearance. With His large harem of beautiful brides, He loves each of us so much, and makes each of us feel so special in the way that we each need. He whispers in each of our ears saying, "How beautiful is your love, my sister, my [promised] bride! How much better is your love than wine! And the fragrance of your ointments than all spices!" (Song of Solomon 4:10; AMP).

His message of His true love is in His love letter — the Bible. Jesus' love is authentic love. He speaks into our hearts saying, "O, you fairest among women." He praises us and wipes away any insecurity from our being. He helps us to see ourselves as He sees us, because He fearfully and wonderfully made us – His bride. He is attentive to our needs, protection, provisions, and the vision for our marriage with Him.

He causes us to melt in our hearts each time He says, "O you fairest among women" because I am His love and He is mine. I am the "fairest among women."

During my season of trials, I purchased a card with the following words that encouraged my spirit and soul each time I read it. In fact, I kept it in my Bible.

Let Go and Let God

Words of Hope and Encouragement

By Emily Matthews

When you're searching for truth and you can't find your way,
When people don't hear what you're trying to say,
And the answers won't come to the things that you pray ~
It's time to let go and let God...
Let go of the bad and the good will appear
Trust in the knowledge that He's always near,
That answers and choices are always more clear
when you can let go and let God.
Just lift up your hands and surrender your heart,
Tell Him your worries and He'll do His part,
Let go of the past and your future will start,
when you finally let go and let God.

Prayer for strength to Let it Go!

May the prayers and faith you have in your relationship
with Jesus Christ carry you through your season(s)
of doubt and pain and lead you to a perfect peace
in Jesus Christ.

Jesus, help me to remember that people and things
come into my life for a reason, season or to stay.
Jesus, help me to discern your purpose for people and
things that comes into my life.

Prayer of Deliverance to Let it Go!

If you are holding onto something that God wants you to release, then it was never intended to stay in your life — Let it Go!

If you are holding onto your past, God said to forget the former things and press toward the mark of the high calling in Christ Jesus – Let it Go!

If you are waddling in your hurts and pains, Jesus said that He will give you a new heart – Let it Go!

If you are holding onto a relationship where someone is not treating you right by celebrating your existence, Jesus said that He will be your friend in the time of need, and that He will supply your need (for right relationships) – Let it Go!

If you are trying to mend a relationship and the person is not cooperating with the reconciliation, Jesus said after you have done all that you can do – stand anyhow, and shake the dust (wickedness) off your feet and walk in love and peace – Let it Go!

If you are angered by someone, Jesus said not to let the sun go down on your wrath and to follow peace with all men – Let it Go!

If you are harboring negative and evil thoughts about someone, Jesus said that whatsoever things are lovely, pure, and of an honest report – to think on these things and to cast down every vain imagination – Let it Go!

If you are involved in a substance abuse relationship with illegal drugs, promiscuous sex, or pornography, Jesus said that he will wash you as white as snow – Let it Go!

If you are involved in a job that no longer meets your needs or talents, Jesus said to trust him as He leads you to greener pastures – Let it Go!

If you are simmering inside from a bad attitude, Jesus said to be anxious for nothing, but by prayer and supplication let your requests be made known unto God – Let it Go!

If you are involved in judging and ridiculing others to make yourself look good, Jesus said the same measure that you measure someone else, it shall be measured unto you – Let it Go!

If you are involved in a relationship where the person is not trying to help himself or herself, Jesus said to cast all your cares and burdens upon Him for He loves you – Let it Go!

If you are experiencing stress, anxiety and depression about the cares of this life, Jesus said, "Come unto me all ye that labour and are heavy laden and I will give you rest, take my yoke upon you, and learn of me; for I am meek and lowly in heart: and ye shall find rest unto your souls. For my yoke is easy, and my burden is light." (Matthew 11:28-30, KJV) – Let it Go!

If you are experiencing a situation in your life that you are trying to handle alone and it is not working, Jesus wants you to take your hands off the situation, so that He can work things out for you – Let it Go!

Affirmative of My Belief

I believe that God is trying to do a new thing in my life.

I believe that I am God's child and property—Jesus said that I am a royal priesthood.

I believe that all things work together for my good because I am of those that love the Lord and called according to His purpose.

Now that you think better of yourself—with the thoughts that Christ wants for His bride—you can let it go! Jesus has something better for you. You must continue to release all of your life into His hands, because He can handle every situation. He knows your beginning from your end.

It is obvious from life's situations that we cannot handle many of life's problems, but He can. We must never go back to take on what we have let go. Let it go, so that He can bring you into your Promised Land to enjoy your inheritance.

About the Author

Dr. Virginia Harrison is a multi-gifted motivational speaker, teacher, and author. She is the founder and president of Kingdom of God Ministries Incorporated and Virginia Harrison Ministries International Incorporated. In pursuit of fulfilling God's plan for her life, she experienced hardship, disappointments, hurts, and depression and learned that she had to let go of the negative feelings inside to move forward in the plan of God for her life (Jeremiah 29:11; KJV). Dr. Harrison is included in the World's Who's Who of Women, Who's Who in the World International, Who's Who of Professional Women, Who's Who in the East, Who's Who in Women in America, and Who's Who in the South and Southeast, Strathmore Who's Who in America, Who's Who of American Women, Metropolitan Who's Who, and Madison Who's Who. She has earned her Associates of Art in Business Management, Prince George's Community College (MD); Diploma in the Advanced Ministerial Program, National Bible Institute (MD); Bachelor of Arts in Religious Education, Washington Saturday College (DC); Bachelor of Science in Organizational Management, Nyack College (DC); Master in Religious Education, Washington Saturday College (DC); Doctorate in Christian Education, Faith Christian University & Schools (MD); Doctorate in Counseling, International Seminary (FLA), and a Diploma in Leadership (Executive Leadership Program), Graduate School (U.S. Department of Agriculture – DC). Dr. Harrison enjoys reading, preaching and traveling.

Breinigsville, PA USA
07 January 2010

230215BV00002B/2/P

9 781615 795468